Dedicated to the memory of
Nathan Asiimwe

"Arise, shine, for your light has come,
and the glory of the Lord rises upon you."
Isaiah 60:1 (NIV)

Acknowledgements

My thanks are due to:

The Lord for saving me and allowing me to experience so much in His service.

My late Mum, for your love and your sensitivity, when you encouraged me to invite your Saviour into my life that night. It was exactly the right question at exactly the right time.

Dad, for all your practical support, not least the use of the farm pickup for such an extended period during the Across Ireland Cross Walk summer.

Pastor Mike Vickers, for coming to Ireland and calling in Richhill; for your inspiration but not your forgetfulness – you left your cross behind you. If I had only known...!

Rachel-Ann Bleakney and Tracey Bell for the incredibly painstaking, dedicated approach and eye for detail you both have. I appreciate the labour of love and long hours that you put into this book and the fight to make it happen – the battle of the book will go down in history for all three of our lives. I couldn't have done any of this without you both. Thank you for standing shoulder to shoulder with me!

Paul and Tricia Andrews for the very generous loan of your caravan, allowing us invaluable flexibility in determining where and when we would lay our head each night. You have been wonderful friends.

Alan Jones, Andy Magwood and Chris Downes for your extended commitment in carrying

the cross with me. It could never have happened without you.

For travelling long distances to support and encourage and cater for the Cross Walk Team - Gillian Glass, Lynne Lockhart and Claire Holmes - Ta.

Richhill Elim – to the Church Leadership Team for your support and leading one of our weekend services for the duration of the walk; to many from the Fellowship who called to help carry the cross and to encourage and bless us on our travels; to the intercessors for upholding us – so appreciated and oh, so necessary!

Praying friends from all over who called and texted so many encouragements at so many crucial times.

My lovely family for your flexibility; to Ben and Anna for just being themselves; to my wonderful wife Denise, who released me for so much of the summer of 2011 to walk the walk; who managed to get me safely from various legs of the walk to our son Christopher's wedding and back, to our daughter Laura's graduation and back, for all the packing and unpacking of cases and caravan, and the rapid wardrobe turnarounds to help ensure the hectic schedule stayed on course! Thanks for allowing me to serve God and for serving alongside me over this last two decades.

The late Nathan Asiimwe for being my friend – I miss you.

Clive Wilson

Contents

Reason for Writing

In the early hours of Monday morning 30th January 2012, I was in my old bedroom in the house in which I grew up. I was brought up on a dairy farm near Richhill in County Armagh, Northern Ireland. My mother Gladys Wilson was born in that same house, known to all as "The Desert", on New Year's Day 1933; she lived there all her life and it was from there on New Year's Day 2012 that she departed to be with Jesus. And so it was that on alternate nights my brother Angus and I stayed to help our Dad through those first few weeks.

I used to visit my parents every Sunday evening after church. With Mum, a late bird like me, it was a chance to have some uninterrupted time. She was a great listener, well read and always encouraged us as children to discover the world around us by asking questions. As a Pastor in our local Elim church, my Sundays were always filled with asking how everyone was and how they and their families were doing. Mum always asked me. A month of Sunday nights had passed in silence.

It had been a very difficult period at the turn of the year when I had to conduct four funerals in just eight days. Marie McCarthy (one of my oldest parishioners and a wonderful prayer warrior), Philip Riddell (an Irish Motorbike Classics Champion, who had just joined the church) and my Mum's funeral all followed in rapid succession to the first death in that week – early on Boxing morning, a close colleague and best friend, Nathan Asiimwe, also said goodbye to Ireland. He was one of the godliest men I have ever had the privilege to know. Originally from Uganda, he had travelled here with his heart burning with the love of God and for people. His heart was for reconciliation. Nathan made no distinctions; a friend to all and a good one.

I was awoken and stirred by a stream of thoughts that came in very quick succession; that this book needed to be written; that it needed to be written by the 23rd April and that it should be dedicated to the memory of Nathan Asiimwe.

It was very clear and very concise; I had no idea whatsoever of the significance of 23rd April other than I knew it wasn't very far away! I also knew I had absolutely no qualifications whatsoever to be an author, other than perhaps I might have a story to tell. The author Jeffrey Archer once alluded to the fact that everyone had at least one story in them!

This is mine – a story of a 430 mile journey on foot across the island of Ireland in the summer of 2011. "Why on earth would anyone want to do that?" you may well ask!

Where do I start?

Everything these days, in our modern online world, seems to start with the prefix "www." This is very much an 'off-line' story but, in keeping with modern times, it still has a "www" introduction.

It is...

A story of the **Word** – God's

A story of the **Walk** – Through this His Land

A story of the **Ways** – Gods' and our highways

Word

Allow me to share how God revealed His power through two key verses from His Word that we have had the privilege to watch at work changing both lives and locations throughout our land.

Isaiah 45:8 *"Rain down, you heavens, from above and let the skies pour down righteousness; Let the earth open, let them bring forth salvation and let righteousness spring up together. I, the Lord, have created it" (NKJV).*

Jeremiah 22:29 *"O Land, land, land. Hear the word of the Lord" (NIV).*

Walk

Allow me to invite you to join me as we walk together some 430 miles across the length and breadth of this beautiful island.

Ways

Watch with me the wonderful ways of God along the highways and byways of Ireland, both North and South.

I trust that you too will be blessed as you walk this walk with me and, as you read this account of the journey which was birthed in Uganda, that you will journey with me into more than just the Irish countryside and will get something of a small glimpse into the spiritual heritage of this nation, its past, its present and its future as shared through the lives of some very ordinary men and women I met along the way. I trust and pray that God blesses this story to your heart and encourages you in your walk through life and that you too will feel encouraged to release God's righteousness and salvation in the midst of your own homes and villages and towns and cities and this His land and beyond, as He directs.

You want... whaaat?

"I want you to come to Uganda with me."

This statement was put to me in November 2010 by one of my best friends, Nathan Asiimwe, over the telephone line. He wanted me to preach with him at a Pastors' Conference in Rushere, Uganda. "But Nathan, I have no desire to go to Uganda, nor do I have the money to go and anyhow, I believe I am called to Ireland!" was my immediate reply. Many times in the past, I had listened to Nathan's wisdom and insights and knew him sufficiently well enough not to put the telephone down quite as quickly as one may be tempted to. I listened a little longer.

He explained that someone else had offered to go and could fund their trip but, despite this, he felt strongly prompted to encourage me to join him on this specific trip. Still mindful of my more local calling, I recalled what Ray Cotter, the Elim Missions Director in Ireland had once told me. He said that to travel to minister and see God at work in other parts of the world would, rather than depriving my home church, actually enrich us all as a result. This was an insight that would show itself true through my experience.

Nathan spoke. I listened. We discussed practicalities and figures. I didn't have the estimated £1000 for a flight. As I spoke, the letterbox in our house rattled. I walked to the door, phone in hand, to find an envelope on the mat simply addressed "Clive – for your work". The envelope contained £100. I laughed and said, "Nathan, I just...perhaps...possibly... might be going to Uganda. I have just received the tithe of exactly the amount needed for the flight – the rest might follow!"

I began praying with a more open mind. I asked God about the trip with Nathan, about timing and about His provision. It quickly became apparent that Nathan had been right, the idea for the trip had been right, the funds were available and, for the first time in my life, I would find myself in the continent of Africa.

Africa was awash with colour, scenery and smiles. Everywhere we went we met extraordinary people.

I stood in the middle of the world, straddling the equator. It was a pleasure to travel with Nathan who, though battling significant health issues, was a perfect host.

Over the course of the next two weeks he regaled me with many cultural insights that kept this Irish novice from tramping all over toes and hearts. I protested on the very first day when young people were asked to carry my weighty suitcase, but was quietly told that this is Nathan's Africa and I must learn to learn and learn to listen. I protested that it was unfair for them in the heat to be so burdened. He turned to face me and asked, "Do you want to waste your time at the Conference preaching to the trees?" Somewhat baffled, I asked what he meant and heard his wise words: "In my culture you must let people serve and do their bit to bless you and if they are allowed to do that then, when you come to share God's word with them, they will be prepared to listen to what you have to say". I said nothing more and bowed to his local knowledge and cultural nous.

As we walked African soil, Nathan shared so many stories of his past, how as a child he looked after the cows for his father and also how he was miraculously healed from a life-threatening heart condition. As a young man, Nathan's spiritual heart was awakened to the sound of the claims upon it by his Saviour, Jesus Christ of Nazareth. Following his decision to worship Jesus, he would look after his cows by day and by night he climbed the hill in his local town, Rushere, to pray in the Anglican Church at the top of the hill. As a gesture of appreciation, he would brush the floor. The Brothers Grimm tale "The Elves and the Shoemaker" tells the story of a poor shoemaker who left some leather on his bench to sew up the next morning and to

his surprise when he arrived in his workshop he found the job was already completed and the shoes stood ready to sell. The industrious elves completed their work before daybreak and unselfishly worked undiscovered. After many nights, the shoe-maker and his wife hid themselves away to uncover the benefactors, to whom they owed a huge debt of gratitude for helping reverse their ailing fortunes. Just as the elves had hurried away every night (until that final night) before they were discovered, so too Nathan would disappear at first light, closing the door to begin his daily chores once more. Nathan's grasp of the Great Commission, this 'sending out' of the gospel, was something that never left him. As a young boy he watched planes flying overhead and believed that one day he would travel further than his home nation to tell people of his Jesus.

Faithfulness to God led to an invitation to speak at a Youth With A Mission (YWAM) conference in Scandinavia, where he was extended a further invitation to the United Kingdom to inaugurate a Discipleship Training Programme. This he did in Banbridge, Co. Down, with the help of his new Irish bride, Annmarie from Limerick. It was during his early years in Ireland that he and I first met and where I heard of his passion for the gospel and its effective communication through the use of modern media. With the Discipleship Training Programme running successfully, he and Annmarie turned their attention to their vision of setting up a community radio station with a Christian ethos. That dream was eventually fulfilled and the radio station called Shine FM was born.

Not content with a radius of 12 miles of listening ears around Banbridge, Nathan launched Internet broadcasting with Voice of Peace Radio Broadcasts, reaching many countries immediately around his beloved Uganda. His weekly broadcasts became unmissable for many, many people. Countless stories of lives coming to faith made their way back to Ireland. The radio broadcasts led to the need for a Teaching Conference for local pastors in Uganda. It was to meet this very request that Nathan had asked me to accompany him.

We flew from Dublin to Amsterdam on Monday 10th January 2011 and onward to Entebbe airport, continuing west on the dusty roads to Rushere. Our Conference ran from Thursday 13th through to Sunday 16th, during which time we ministered to several hundred church leaders and many others from a very wide catchment area.

The theme we were encouraged to centre our messages around was the thought from Genesis 18:14 – "Is anything too hard for the Lord?" (KJV). The meetings were lively, the worship extraordinary.

The engagement of the people, the willingness to seamlessly switch the lead worship role, the energy to stand, to dance, to praise God long into the night, left me enthralled and not a little exhausted. I remember standing to preach one day and saying, "I don't know very much but, if you ask me, when we get to Heaven it wouldn't surprise me that one of the main worship leaders is an African!" Whilst I was unable to understand many of the words they sang, the delight in those worship sessions was so impacting I expect never to forget it.

During the four-day conference we stayed in the guesthouse of the local Rushere Community Hospital, where our breakfast one morning was interrupted by an American nurse. She walked across to our table and, without any introduction, began a long (and probably justified) tirade about the standard of nursing care at the local community hospital at the foot of the hill. She described the attitude of the nurses - they didn't seem to care whether a patient lived or died.

She explained how infection rates were unacceptable, nursing morale was poor and even the local community thought carefully before they would avail of its services! She later introduced herself simply as Florence and, as she walked away, I thought of the only other Florence known for nursing — Florence Nightingale. She left the breakfast table with such negativity that, I'll admit, I felt the pair were poles apart. That said, as she walked away, I felt strongly the need to pray for the hospital.

The meetings in Africa differed from Ireland in more ways than the worship! Amongst the differences were interruptions from a threatening visitor - an intrusion into the back of one of the tents by a deadly snake. This, as you might imagine, engendered a great deal of fear and concern for all close by. It came as a shock to the locals too, who admitted to never having seen a snake cross the open ground into a crowd. On this occasion, however, a python did just that, causing much consternation until it was duly dispatched and the meeting could resume.

On the final night of the Conference, Nathan and I visited the hospital where its Administrator greeted us and asked how he could be of assistance. Nathan explained to him that we were there to pray for the hospital, to which he replied, "Ah, two pastors - you are here to pray for the sick!" Nathan tried to explain what I had felt - that we were not there to pray for the sick per se, but to pray for the hospital. After not a little confusion and frustration on everyone's

part, my request, to be taken to the strategic decision-making centre of the hospital, remained unfulfilled. The closing scene in this comedy of confusion was one of us, on our knees in the adjoining chapel, praying the words of Isaiah 45:8 on its floor –
"Rain down, you heavens, from above and let the skies pour down righteousness; Let the earth open, let them bring forth salvation and let righteousness spring up together. I, the Lord, have created it" (NKJV).

We were interrupted by the Administrator. "You will NOW pray for the sick!" he announced. We enquired as to whom had the greatest need and he led us to a dying man suffering from the grave effects of skin cancer. It was a privilege to pray with him and lead his grandson to the Lord. As we walked up the hill away from the hospital towards our accommodation, I said to Nathan "We did not do what we were meant to tonight." Nathan knew that too. He had tried to explain to the Administrator our exact intention, but couldn't convince him to grant the request. It seemed a frustrating end to what had been an otherwise incredible four days of ministry.

Divine Appointments
Two nights later, on the final night before we left Rushere, we were invited by Wilson (a man who was setting up a new hardware shop in town) for an evening meal. Our host was alone until we were joined midway

through our evening meal by his wife. She had just returned from Kenya after burying her father. She set down her suitcases and joined us as we recounted the previous few days events at the conference. We eventually concluded with our frustrating visit to Rushere Community Hospital. She asked what I was doing at the hospital and I explained that I was looking for the strategic decision-making centre of the hospital but had been thwarted in that search. She was amazed and said, "Clive, ten months ago I was appointed the Chief Executive Officer of Rushere Community Hospital. What the American nurse told you is all true and I am struggling to know what to do to change things. It is amazing you are in my home because the wall that you are sitting with your back to right now is the wall of the boardroom of the hospital! A few months ago I moved it up here!"

In less than five minutes we were on our knees on the boardroom floor praying the words of Isaiah 45:8. **I had discovered in my very short period of time in Africa that, although it is a vast continent, Almighty God is able to lead people with extraordinary precision. We left the house praising God and in awe of His all-knowing, all-seeing planning.**

During my time in Uganda the Holy Spirit impressed upon me to study in the book of Genesis. This I did. What I was about to read was to make such a significant impact on my thinking that, had I known then what I know now, I might have chosen to study any book other than Genesis!

Starting at Genesis 13, I began to re-read the story of Lot and Abram, of how they were struggling with too many herdsmen and copious numbers of camels and cattle. To avoid further escalation of conflict between quarrelling herdsmen, Abram offered Lot a choice – "If you go the left then I will go to the right or if you take the right then I will go to the left" (Genesis 13:9 ESV). Lot chose all the well watered plains of the Jordan Valley and journeyed East to pitch his tent near Sodom. After Lot had departed, God said to Abram "Lift up now your eyes and look from the place where you are northward and southward and eastward and westward for all the land which you see I will give it to you and your offspring for ever." (Genesis 13: 14-15 ESV). Skipping a verse, I arrived at the instruction God then gave Abram when He told him to "arise, walk through the length and breadth of the land for I will give it to you" (Genesis 13:17 ESV).

For some time I mused on the fact that God had required Abram to walk the length and breadth of the land, even though it had already been given to him. "Why Lord," I asked, "If You had already given it to him, did You require him to walk the length and breadth of the land?" That thought, its question and answer was to weigh heavily upon me in the coming months, long after the African sun had set on that balmy evening.

As we packed up and headed back to Kampala to speak at a Conference the following weekend, again the Lord impressed upon me the need to pray at the seat of government in the Nation. I asked Nathan if it was possible for us to access the Houses of Parliament. Although surprised at the request, a few phone calls and several divine appointments later, we found ourselves in the main debating chamber of the Houses of Parliament. Our dedicated guide, who had been specifically appointed to us, was waxing very lyrical on the history of his country and the likely projected outcome of the forthcoming elections. When we asked him if it might be possible for us to pray a blessing on his Parliament and people, he kindly granted us permission and again we prayed the faithful words of Isaiah 45:8 –

"Rain down, you heavens, from above and let the skies pour down righteousness; Let the earth open, let them bring forth salvation and let righteousness spring up together. I, the Lord, have created it" (NKJV).

What subsequently unfolded on national television was intriguing. We were the guests of a man who worked for the Government and often dealt with politicians. Engrossed in National News broadcasts, he relayed to us what had been happening in the days after we had stepped into the Parliament Building. Members of Parliament had started to arrive at the Parliament Buildings carrying millions of Ugandan shillings in plastic bags. The first

MP to do this indicated that the money had been paid directly into her personal bank account by the outgoing Government for 'electioneering' purposes. She declared that this amounted to nothing more than a bribe and needed to be returned. She issued a challenge to her colleagues to follow her example. Isaiah 45:8 speaks of righteousness being released; people doing the right thing. Our host in Kampala, intuitively au fait with a long history of questionable African leaders, asked us what on earth we had done in the Houses of Parliament! We had prayed to the Living God. God's word never returns void.

I left Uganda with very happy memories of an amazing trip with an extraordinary individual in the person of Nathan Asiimwe and his precious family. His sister Flora and brother-in-law Pastor Patrick had raised some 11 children, two choirs of talented children that, whether asked to sing or to wash, iron or deliver shirts by 7.30am the following day, always did what was needed with enthusiasm and an ever present smile.

I also left with the unresolved question as to Abram's quest - to walk the length and breadth of his land. February, March and April bore the question more heavily as it gained gravitas each month. I shared it with the Church Working Group at Richhill Elim Church and with our congregation. **I felt God wanted me to complete a similar journey: to walk the length and breadth of Ireland. Mindful of the miles we had to cover, all I could say to them, and to God, was "I am so glad I wasn't born in Canada or Russia!"** When they asked how exactly I intended to achieve that objective and exactly what I proposed to do on such a trip I reminded them of a visitor that we had had to the church in 2009...

Nathan with his sister and brother-in-law

A Significant Stranger

I was invited by a committee of ministers from Portadown to preach at the 150th anniversary of the 1859 revival arriving in the town. The event was to take place in the meadows alongside the River Bann where, all those years ago, some young men travelled from County Antrim to relate their accounts of the extraordinary move of God in the North of the Province. On that occasion, hundreds of people were on their faces in the meadows before God as His Holy Spirit worked conviction in the hearts and lives of men and women.

I had no idea why they would ask a pastor of a small village church nearby to share with them, knowing there were many others more closely linked with Portadown and its history than me. It soon became evident, however, that it might just have been because they all knew that it was going take place very early on a Saturday morning outdoors in less than ideal weather conditions and Clive wasn't that bright! That said, I was glad to be there and despite notes being blown all over the place (my wife Denise, as always, came to my rescue) we talked of revival once more.

I told them that I believed revival was once again on the agenda for Ireland. In fact, I had just heard from a close friend that a travelling pastor from England, whilst journeying up through Ireland, had borne a promise of revival in his heart. I hoped to meet him within the next few days.

Preaching at the Meadows at the 150th Anniversary of the Revival arriving in Portadown

17

My first contact with Pastor Mike Vickers came through a phone call from a friend, Alison Calvin, who worked with the Church of Ireland in Cavan. She explained that she had driven past a man carrying a 12 foot high cross and thought he was a bit 'wacky'. Nonetheless she turned her car around and spoke with him. That conversation convinced her that he was a 'good guy' and she asked us to give him a bed for the night when he reached Armagh. I agreed and, on 13th July 2009 (which was really the Twelfth that year – it's a Northern Irish thing!), the anticipated visit from Pastor Vickers arrived. He asked if I could collect him from the police cordon that had closed the road for the parade. It was late afternoon and the District Lodges were returning back into town from 'the field' after celebrating the Twelfth Day on the 13th.

We shared an evening meal together and listened to his vision, God's call evident upon his life. Mike had been involved in the establishment and development of two churches in England. More recently, though, he had felt directed by the Lord to a more itinerant ministry. Having accepted this new venture, he was eventually led to walk from Scotland to Brighton with a Crown flag (which depicts Jesus as True Leader) and from the East Coast of England to St David's in Wales with a 12 foot cross. Whilst finishing his walk at the beach at St David's, someone from his London-based team asked if his years of walking were over, to which he replied, "Hopefully!"

Within a few months, however, he felt the Holy Spirit urge him to study and pray over a map of Ireland. Having done so, he felt strongly to come to Ireland in the summer of 2009 and, bearing the cross, he traversed Galway to Bangor, County Down, a diagonal South West-North East journey across Ireland. Before commencement in Galway, Mike felt prompted by the Holy Spirit to surrender his wallet to his team from England, explaining that he felt God was saying "This one has to be done by faith." His team protested saying, "Mike, you don't know anyone in Ireland; how will you survive without contacts and places to stay?"

Mike with the cross.

Despite their protestations Mike headed north. After many twists and turns along the road he and his blistered feet made it to a chemist's shop in Roscommon. Whilst there getting his feet patched, the attendee said, "You really should be off those feet

for 36 hours to give them a chance to heal" and proffered him a telephone contact. After calling it, Mike discovered that it was the number for the Roscommon base of Operations Mobilisation (OM) Mission, an international Christian missions movement equipping people to share God's love and strengthen and plant churches. They came to collect him within 20 minutes. He was given a bed for the night and spent the next day sharing with their team. Whilst there, the OM Ireland National Director (Mike Mullins) telephoned to ask Pastor Mike what exactly he had been doing. Having explained his vision and purpose in Ireland. Mike Mullins revealed that he had also felt there needed to be a Cross Walk in Ireland and his team were on the first leg of their walk from Cork to Roscommon, in the centre of the country. **The question was asked: "Do you think just perhaps, possibly, God is in this?" It was a rhetorical question.**

When Mike stayed in our house, we felt we should do something to help; more specifically to buy his flight home. After a little discussion and an attempt to work out the probable end date of his journey, we purchased a flight from Belfast to Gatwick.

Subsequent to that decision, Mike was very quiet and later as I offered to walk with him and help shoulder the cross for the day on the 13th (which was really the 14th - still a Northern Irish thing!) he told me that he had something to share with Denise and

myself. He said a retired gentleman, who was a professional rambler and who regularly organised his itinerary (knowing all the good and reasonably priced places to stay) asked Mike, "HOW are we going to get you home from Ireland and HOW are we going to get the cross home?" Mike informed him that a few nights previous to that question being asked he had had a dream - the cross would stay in Ireland for evangelism purposes and an Elim Pastor would buy his flight home! His old seasoned Christian colleague jested, "Those Elim boys are rarely in the spirit! – I will send a rowboat across the Irish Sea to collect you!" When he discovered the eventual outworking of God's precise planning he, like us, enjoyed the mirth of the moment and stood in awe of our awesome God.

The offer to walk with Mike and shoulder the burden for the day was made on the clear proviso that he would bring the cross onto the top of the hill in our local village. After we'd talked to many people along the way, we eventually arrived, midday, at the top of the hill of Richhill village. Pastor Vickers read from his Bible in the presence of some believers from almost every church in the village. He read a promise Jesus gave to his disciples: "After this the Lord appointed seventy-two others and sent them on ahead of him, two by two, into every town and place where he himself was about to go" Luke 10:1 (ESV).

Mike shared that he had walked with a revival promise for Ireland, but every single mile from Galway to Armagh he had walked on his own. He declared that if the promise for revival was for anywhere in Ireland it was for Richhill because today, for the first time, he had walked into the village together with me.

I was amazed at that promise. I thought back to the first night when I was a pastor in the local Elim church at the bottom of that same hill. The Bible study that night had focused on Joshua crossing the Jordan River and selecting memorial stones to build an altar to remember it. I gathered the church members in a circle and I prayed that the hill of Richhill would really be a standing stone in the County. That was at 9pm. A few hours later, the son of one of my longest serving employees in the factory took his own life on a tree at the very top of the hill within the Castle grounds. It was devastating blow for the family and for the community. It felt to me a little like the enemy throwing down a gauntlet and saying, "I will give you the headlines out of Richhill that I think you deserve." It was not what we deserved. It was not what we wanted.

On the journey into Richhill I was struck by the sight of one of the most visual signs in our created world – a rainbow, given as a reminder that our God, from the outset, has always been a God of promise. I stopped to take a photograph.

And so, I told the Church Working Group - the cross that we now babysat in the church roof space, the one that had arrived at the top of the hill in our village along with such a significant promise of revival, would now come on a journey with us!

A Second String to the Bow

Whilst I could envisage evangelising those who would engage with us on our journey walking through Ireland with a cross, the key objective was to release two (very dynamic it turned out) scriptures into the heart of every town and village along our route.

As I preached at that anniversary of the 1859 revival in Portadown, one of the local pastors sensed the Holy Spirit saying to him that revival doesn't always come in exactly the same way every time and that, if we would seek Him, we would be given a key.

On Friday afternoons in the subsequent weeks, times of prayer were held and over the weeks two verses were increasingly impressed upon our thinking, the first of which we prayed in Africa:

Isaiah 45:8

"Rain down, you heavens, from above and let the skies pour down righteousness; Let the earth open, let them bring forth salvation and let righteousness spring up together. I, the Lord, have created it" (NKJV).

The second verse was:

Jeremiah 22:29

"O Land, land, land. Hear the word of the Lord" (NIV).

Praying those verses in certain areas seemed to be a bit like asking planet earth to go back and do what it was originally designed to do - work for the kingdom of Heaven. As we began to pray them in both domestic and city settings, we began to notice a difference.

One example at household level of the power of Isaiah 45:8 was when the Holy Spirit impressed upon me to pray those verses in a house in the County. I did that with the owner's agreement and left the home. Within a few days, the police came knocking at the house searching for controlled drugs. They searched the property from top to bottom but found none, but what they did find at the electricity meter box was a device for slowing down the meter reading and thereby the magnitude of the monthly bill. The police demanded an explanation from the owner the following day at the police station. The explanation: the owner of the property had a son who set up a gym at the back of his father's property. In the midst of a very cold winter at the start of 2011, he told his father not to worry about the cost of the electricity bill caused by him and his mates training. His father was also warned that, should he touch one of their devices, he would be punished. His father, a relatively new follower of Jesus, knew of the violent tendencies of his son and often lost sleep over the issue. He knew what was happening was illegal but also of the potential repercussions of removing the device.

Isaiah 45:8 hits the floor of the property. The device is removed. The back bill is paid to the Northern Ireland Electricity Board and all charges dropped. Because of the way it happened, the son had no reason to implicate his father, who could sleep soundly once again. **Righteousness was restored.**

On a visit with our oldest daughter Laura to Newcastle upon Tyne, we felt we should pray in the centre of her new city where she was studying at University. The first day we were there was the final bank holiday in August and the day had come to an end without us achieving our objective. Laura reminded me, "Dad, you still haven't prayed in town." The next day, at around 11 o'clock, I felt impressed to go to the Lord Earl Grey statue in the centre of the city. Unlike the previous day, when no one was around, there was an open-air meeting already taking place. Microphones were set up, guitarists played and a group of reformed alcoholics shared the gospel message. I listened to them sing and then approached one of the group members, tapping him on the shoulder, and asked if he would read something for me. He spent the next song, I guessed, pondering what exactly I wanted him to do. He sauntered in my direction and questioned me: "You mean read verses from the Bible?" "Exactly," I replied, "Isaiah 45:8 and Jeremiah 22:29." He left to get his Bible and returned to look me squarely in the eye and queried, "Who are you?" I told him I was a pastor from Ireland. Unable to let the issue go he

reiterated the question, "No, but who are you really?" I asked why he was so intent on knowing who I was and he replied that it was simply because "My Bible opened at Isaiah 45:8!" I smiled and said, "Well then, why are you wasting time talking to me? Get on the microphone and read out those verses." When he had finished reading the two verses out over his microphone I thanked him saying, "I know you didn't do that with very much faith or conviction but I believe you have spoken a wonderful blessing over your city today. Thank you for being obedient."

I told the Working Group that I felt the objective God had given me was to pray those two strategic verses at the centre of every town and village we passed through - throughout the length and breadth of the land. It was agreed that we move the project through to implementation.

Preparation

Discussion with close family and friends about what we were about to embark on tended to result in a typical response: "You're going to do what?" Somewhat more encouraging and practical advice resulted from reading Arthur Blessitt's "The Cross" in which he offered the advice: "A journey of a thousand miles begins with a single step."

To navigate the length and breadth of Ireland was, thankfully, not 1000 miles. It was still, however, a substantial undertaking for an amateur! Several years previous, in a marquee one Sunday afternoon in the grounds of the Castle in Richhill, I recall vividly superimposing a cross over the nation of Ireland. That day I placed its intersection over Richhill, a small village near Armagh City.

The visual image stuck with me and, when considering how to traverse Ireland in 2011, the image of the East to West and North to South lines intersecting over Armagh, the ecclesiastical capital of Ireland, was impressed upon me.

Given that we were already busy with our eldest son's wedding and our eldest daughter's

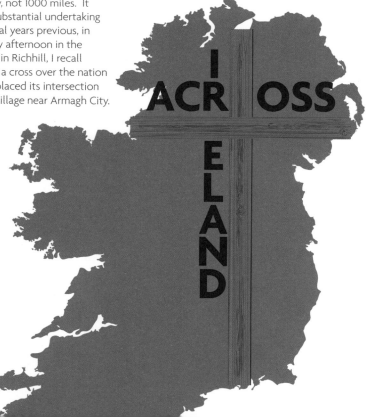

graduation, I attempted to break the Across Ireland Cross Walk into four stages, each with its starting point from the sea simply on based on a straight line due North, South, East and West from Armagh.

Leg 1   Sligo to Armagh
Leg 2   Portrush to Armagh
Leg 3   Strangford to Armagh
Leg 4   Waterford to Armagh

The first three legs could each be achieved in a Monday to Friday timeframe, but the final leg would take place over a fortnight. I wanted to see the Across Ireland Cross Walk completed in a clockwise direction with the three short legs in the North being completed first. My wishful thinking was that by the time it came to the longer final leg, walking boots, and the legs in them, would be well broken in!

In addition to these logistics, I was mindful that when praying around something it is always good to do it a clockwise direction. Often the opposition in the occult world will reverse things (e.g. upside down crosses) and do things in an anticlockwise direction.

Bit by bit, a rough plan began to form. What was needed now was a team and backup support to ensure the project could be completed within the allotted time.

During the month of May, I spoke with one of our congregation members, Mr Alan Jones. He was on holiday at the time and

I asked if he'd fancy joining me for a walk through Ireland. To his credit, he didn't hang up - but then that is the beauty of texting! I outlined what I was thinking and asked if he would like to accompany me on the journey. He said the text was timely as he was on a holiday break and had time to reflect on the fact that many years ago he felt something of that nature needed to be done in Ireland but, until now, he had never had the opportunity. A resounding YES resulted and Alan, who spent much of his life in leadership and project management, doubled the team size and I now had a logistics manager in place! Many others were to join the walk but in particular Christopher Downes and Andy Magwood committed many consecutive days and sometimes weeks to help us attain our objective.

I wanted as many people as possible to join me on the walk. Finding accommodation for one individual and stranger is one thing but to expect Irish hospitality to extend to two or three beds every night might prove logistically complicated to find and fund. As we prayed, we thought that a caravan might just be the answer. The only problem was that we didn't own a caravan nor did we have a vehicle that could tow a caravan.

Whilst we didn't own a caravan we had, for several years, borrowed a caravan from close family friends and by way of some small recompense we used to overwinter it in one of the farm sheds.

This caravan was truly spiritual. It had only ever gone to Christian festivals - three in all, a bit like the Old Testament requirement to visit Jerusalem three times a year for pilgrimages for Passover, the Feast of Weeks (Pentecost or Shavuot) and Tabernacles (Sukkot). The caravan provided accommodation at Summer Madness (a youth event staged in the RUAS Balmoral by the Church of Ireland Church), at Elim Hillsborough Bible week and at the Methodist Bible week held every year in Castlewellan. This year however, for the first time in 21 years, Hillsborough Bible week was not happening and the caravan was not needed for either of the other two events.

As a result, our dear friends Paul and Tricia Andrews kindly granted us the use of their caravan. My dad also graciously released the farm pick-up to provide the necessary horsepower for as long as was required. Both of these provisions proved invaluable to the Cross Walk team's ability to remain flexible and ready for all occasions. To the onlooker, we may have appeared as an unconventional travelling family. This would no doubt lead to more than a little bemusement along the way and was, most likely, the key reason as to why we would later during our journey be evicted from beside a church late one evening!

Set with our motley band of pilgrims, it was time to follow this trail - the trail of the cross.

The night before the long walk after! On my right, Alan Jones, our Logistics Manager from Dollingstown and on my left, a fresh faced but soon to be tired Chris Downes from Coleraine.

Ballyconnell

Enniskillen

Armagh

Monaghan

A Walk from the West

CROSS WALK LEG 1
Ballyconnell, Co Sligo to Armagh City

CROSS WALK LEG 1
Ballyconnell, Co Sligo to Armagh City

MONDAY 20TH JUNE

We had left Richhill late on the Sunday after the evening service to overnight in Manor Hamilton and, whilst it was the intention of the logistics manager that we begin at 6am after a hearty breakfast, we eventually made it to Ballyconnell, Co. Sligo and the walk began at the water's edge at 9am!

In an interview with Margaret Brown on Ocean FM that morning, I shared about the task in hand. **The magnitude that the challenge posed had become all too apparent to me the previous evening as we drove west from Richhill to Co. Sligo. Every road mile I drove west I thought, "We have to walk ALL this back again!"**

My Bible reading before starting out that morning was from Genesis 43:11 when Jacob, who somewhat reluctantly was sending his sons on a journey back to Egypt, said "If it *must* be so, then do this."

I prayed: "Lord, all I know is that You want this done and it will be done in Your strength and in Your Name. Help us as a team to be faithful to the very end."

DIVERSION

AN EARLY OBSTACLE

We decided to take our 430 mile journey each carrying the cross in half mile stints. When I went to do my second lift, we came around the corner to be faced with a diversion sign. **Sligo County Council had closed the road and one of the local workmen informed me that I would be re-routed by some significant distance.**

Despite my protestations that I had only a single wheeler, there was no leeway whatsoever! "If I let you go down there," he said, "my supervisor will turn you back after a couple of miles - you picked the wrong week to do a Cross Walk!" The de-tour resulted in us walking along the edge of Sligo Bay;

That detour introduced me to a strong visual image, that of an unusally dry, brown landscape. The trees and hedges looked parched, quite the paradox to the lush green countryside we expect in the Emerald Isle. It stood out as being so unusual and perhaps hinted at a similar sense of drought and lifelessness in the spiritual realm.

AN EXPLOSIVE START

The first fright I had on the crosswalk was what I thought to be a set of air brakes being let off by a quarry lorry that had just passed me. It turned out, however, to be a blowout on the wheel of the cross! No thorns, no glass and a forward speed that averaged 3 mph - now that takes some doing! It seemed to me like someone or something didn't want to see this walk started, never mind completed!

Thankfully our logistics manager had included a solid wheel in our spares for just such an eventuality, though not even he had expected a pit stop quite this soon!

On our first day, we managed to clock up a total, never to be repeated, 31 miles through some spectacular scenery, past a wonderful waterfall and a picturesque lake to lunch beside.

Chris and Alan pictured on our journey from the West.

Enthusiasm abounded. Word experts tell us that our English word 'enthusiasm' is originally derived from the Greek word "entheos" - en meaning "in" & theos "God". It was great to be in the West; it was great to be in a good team; it was great to be underway and it is certainly great to be in God!

Walking 31 miles in one day was not to be repeated on our journey, thankfully! Early enthusiasm was going to have to be tempered with realism. The fast pace of that first day was deliberately maintained as we knew Chris had to leave us for a pre-arranged appointment the next day. The initial drive to keep up a good average was then brought back to a more manageable and sustainable long-term average of approximately 17 miles per day.

TUESDAY 21ST JUNE – MIDSUMMER'S DAY

It was a very wet morning with a fine, soaking rain falling relentlessly. Despite the weather set back and being one man down, we laboured on. Half mile after half mile, Alan and I shared the load with each stint feeling just a wee bit heavier and a wee bit longer. It was stretching. Today felt like it would be a day of just doing it, and we did, along twisty roads with few to engage us or to encourage, until dinner time when Alan spotted a little red car and three very enthusiastic girls waving through the rain. Gillian, Claire and Lynne had joined us from Co. Armagh to cater for and encourage us and join us on our walk. Our spirits lifted at being joined by the girls and their enthusiasm was infectious.

I hadn't thought to text the girls after their offer to come down and meet us as it was setting out to be so very wet, but I was glad they met up with us anyway as we reached the "Imagine Stones"- a sculpture situated on the shore of Lough MacNean, close to the village of Blacklion, Co Cavan.

Whilst at the stones, I had a passing glance at a nearby sign with an image of a dead bird upside down. I had no idea about the inscription; perhaps it harkened back to the site's historical links with a former hunting retreat or possibly indicated fertile waters for wildfowl hunters. Whatever it meant, it certainly seemed incongruous in this beautiful, vibrant environment. As I thought of the bird on its back, I thought also of our land, so often upside down in many ways.

We made it back to Top's garage at Blacklion for lunch, where we enjoyed the leftovers from a fundraiser that my youngest daughter Anna had hosted. Anna was travelling that summer on a Mission trip to Paraguay with a South America team and was raising money to support the work with the young children in Concepcion. Whilst I could not be there, many people contributed that night and I was glad not all of the goodies were consumed by the well-wishers who had come to support her!

I prayed, "Lord, turn this land the right way up! Where there is death, please bring life."

Whilst we were not collecting any money for missions or charity through the walk, from time to time we saw the love of Irish men and women expressed in practical ways. It was at this stop-off that we saw the first provision for our journey. Some Euros were kindly given to us for diesel. We were mindful, too, of the ever present blessings of Dad's pickup truck and Paul and Tricia's caravan and prayed that God would bless them too for so generously releasing their resources into this Cross Walk Project.

The first to volunteer as a cross carrier was a local lady, Eileen. She had been tipped off by her brother who had seen the team in Sligo and rang to say, "There is some eejit walking with a cross and he's heading in your direction." She and some of her friends and neighbours, Mary and John, were on the lookout for us, trying to find out what we were up to. They gave us an opportunity to pray with them and we continue to pray the impact of the cross would bring lasting change.

Someone else who shared their intrigue was Ciarán, a guy sporting a Welsh rugby top. Based upon the myriad of questions he asked, it was clear to see, as Jesus once remarked about an enquirer that came to him that, he was not far from the Kingdom. It was good to be able encourage him on his journey towards faith in Jesus.

400 metres more and we stumbled upon a vehicle worthy of being on the motoring TV show "Top Gear" - a wonderful, top of the range Land Rover in metallic black set against the backdrop of a run-down out-building. We talked with the owner about the joys and pleasure of driving either a black or white vehicle along with the subsequent after-care they demand to stay spotless. We also talked of black and white issues both in life

and eternity. One thing in particular puzzled the man - when he heard I was a Pastor of an Elim church, he enquired how we existed as a denomination without holy water.

The subject of his thoughts and questions about 'holy' water intrigued me as I walked on. I had once heard Alan speaking about a Japanese entrepreneur and author, Masaru Emoto from Japan, whose work revolved around the hypotheses that water could react to different stimuli. He has sold over two million books with various titles, such as "The Secret Life of Water" and "The Hidden Messages in Water", trying to convince the world that there is a discernible difference in the shape of water crystals that have been subjected to music, harsh words or even prayer and selling his water products to the public.

The scientific world remains as yet to be fully

convinced. Nonetheless, it set me thinking as I walked with the ubiquitous Irish rainwater falling all too often upon us - if so much of our human bodies are made up of the key constituent water and Mr Emoto is genuinely on to something, it might add a fraction more understanding to the verse in Proverbs 18:21 that tells us that "death and life are in the power of the tongue" (KJV). It is interesting that scripture places it in that order; death first, as all too often we are prone to say something negative or critical about ourselves more quickly than something positive or encouraging. Maybe if we were to choose our words more carefully, it just might bless others and ourselves and our cells! It was an interesting way to occupy another half mile stint!

Our target for the end of the first day was to walk as far as the Elim Church in Enniskillen. We sent the caravan on ahead of the team with the cross and had it parked alongside the church before we managed to advise the local pastor, Cameron Crawford. Little wonder then, when the caravan was discovered by one of his parishioners, Cameron received a phone call informing him that travellers had taken up residence!

We just had enough time to wolf down the tea the girls had so kindly prepared and quickly change into dry clothes before their mid-week meeting began. The meeting brought great liberty and many opportunities to share and pray with many of the individuals we met. After the midweek service was over we gathered the church members and their pastor, and took the cross to pray in the centre of Enniskillen.

After the meeting, a widow, who hadn't been a follower of Jesus for very long, invited the team for supper and a chance to get showers – bliss!. It was a wonderful Christian gesture, especially given that she had recently slipped and fallen at a community centre "Can't Cook – Won't Cook" fundraiser. The offer may have been due in some small measure to the fact that it was indeed she who had raised the false alarm earlier that afternoon. Imagine her red face when she arrived at her mid-week meeting to discover that the caravan was not one of the travelling community but instead another Elim pastor and his motley crew! She was made to pay for her mistake both during the meeting and afterwards, but she turned out to be a great sport and a wonderful hostess. Showered and suppered we returned to sleep in the grounds of the church.

We brought the cross to the centre of Enniskillen.

WEDNESDAY 22ND JUNE

The next morning, John and Audrey Wilson came on site to cook a wonderful Ulster fry for us to kick off day three of the walk. John, affectionately known to us as Captain Cook, had lost his right hand in an industrial accident. We really appreciated his and Audrey's special efforts on our behalf. The good start to the day was about to be added to when, before leaving the city, Alan prayed with a lady and led her on her way to follow Jesus. In some sense, this was to be a rare delight for the team because as we prayed and released Isaiah 45:8 we usually had to move on to the next place on our journey. On this occasion, praying in the evening and then staying over allowed us the delight of witnessing visible first fruits in Enniskillen. We prayed more would follow, but if indeed there should not be another one in the next 400 miles, it would still all be worth it to win just one soul to Jesus. Proverbs 11:30 informs us that "he who wins souls is wise" (NKJV).

We spent an hour trying to dry clothes by lifting them in and out of the caravan between the showers. As my Uncle Fred used to say, "There was good drying between the showers." He may have been right, but if you had been suffering from vertigo that day - you would have been dizzy by the end of it!

Along the way we met the Rev. David Campbell near Lisnaskea. He waited patiently until we caught up with him and extended an invitation to attend his midweek service at the Independent Methodist church. He had been the pastor for nine years and was interested in our vision.

The next morning, we met David at the Jailhouse Square where we stationed a man on each of the four sides of the Celtic cross which stood at the centre and prayed Isaiah 45: 8 and Jeremiah 22:29.

Rev. David Campbell and myself at the Celtic cross in Lisnaskea.

Along the way we had been invited to stay in the home of Leslie Gray and his wife, from Newtownbutler. Upon arrival we received a hearty Fermanagh welcome to their home. Leslie began the round of introductions by saying that some time ago he had met and hosted a man from England doing something similar to ourselves and that his name was Mike Vickers (adding that we probably hadn't heard of him). He introduced his wife Sheila, adding that it was in our county, Co. Armagh that they had received final confirmation concerning their prayers about whether or not to get married. "It was in a wee church called Richhill Elim," he said, "but you probably haven't heard of it".

I smiled as I introduced our team saying, "The cross sitting against the gable wall of your house is Mike Vicker's cross and I am the Pastor of ... yes you guessed it... that wee Elim church in Richhill!" What a very small world it is in God's Kingdom.

We had a wonderful night of fellowship with that family who very kindly provided us with dinner, shower facilities and a place to park up for the night...and a hearty Irish breakfast too.

THURSDAY 23RD JUNE

The next day we walked on to Clones. **Clones carries a spiritual significance historically as it has borne witness to some memorable developments in the Kingdom of God in Ireland. John Wesley the English cleric and theologian preached here to some three thousand people in the 1770's and one of the very early Methodist churches in the country was established here.**

As we walked into town, men who were drunk shouted obscenities at the cross and the team as we proceeded to the square. Alan was carrying the cross at the time and he responded to their verbal abuse by simply saying, "Today the kingdom of God has drawn near to you".

We prayed at the Celtic cross in front of the Church of Ireland Church in the centre of town, having earlier walked up to high ground to the top of the motte and bailie.

That night in the Creighton Hotel, about 25 believers gathered together (about half of them from the North and half from the South). I asked them to share their stories with us, keenly aware of the identity we share in Christ. New believers, and some old, shared their unique stories of how the Holy Spirit had impacted their lives. There was a wonderful sense of unity within the family of God.

When the meeting was over and we were leaving the city centre, we discovered the men who had shouted obscenities at us earlier, still drunk and sitting outside on a street bench. One of the men revealed that he had been thinking about what had happened earlier that afternoon and that when he returned back to the bar he felt under extreme conviction about how abusively he had acted. Sometimes the presence of the cross simply passing by unannounced can bring the unrepentant to conviction. We were to observe more of this.

Leslie Gray and I in Clones

FRIDAY 24TH JUNE

On Friday morning we started to walk towards Monaghan, where we met several of the local church leaders at the Church of Ireland Cathedral. On that particular day, the town was buzzing with a Blacksmith's Festival.

At 12 o'clock we prayed beside the Bank of Ireland building near the Diamond where, many years before in 1915, Welshman George Jeffreys preached.

Myself and Chris along with Pastor Stephen Matthews, Monaghan Elim, and Paul, who was involved in street outreach in the town.

In 1913, Jeffreys had been invited by the Methodists but when they heard he was a Pentecostal they decided to cancel the booking!

Two years later, however, he did come to preach in extraordinary meetings where the power of God was to be evidenced by all. Jeffreys, who founded the Elim Pentecostal Church, considered those meetings to be

the very origins of the Elim Movement. He later wrote, "I regard Monaghan ... as being the birth place of this work" (georgejeffreysandstephenjeffreys.blogspot. com).

Given what we know about John Wesley in Clones and George Jeffreys in Monaghan, it would seem that this particular part of Ireland contains a source of old wells. Just as Isaac re-opened his father Abraham's wells, could these wells be re-dug spiritually?

Originally I had planned to finish the crosswalk at the oldest cathedral in Armagh city, the ecclesiastical capital of Ireland. When speaking at a Bible School Graduation on the Saturday before commencing Leg 1, I had outlined my intentions for the walk and asked people to pray that it would be concluded in line with God's timetable and the right locations. Immediately after I had finished speaking, someone approached and simply placed a scrap of paper in my hand with the written words 'Navan Fort'.

As the western leg neared completion, I had the growing impression that we did need to conclude all four legs of the walk at Navan Fort, the original site of pagan worship in Ireland.

So Navan Fort it was! The onward journey to Navan Fort in Armagh was endured in heavy rain.

We walked up the west side of the medieval Navan Fort mound and completed the first

leg of the Cross Walk, by praying the words of Isaiah 45:8 and Jeremiah 22:29. Given the strength of the prevailing wind that had started up, Alan and Chris, together, had significant difficulty keeping the cross upright!

We felt we had finished what we had set out to do for Leg 1 of the Cross Walk and as we walked on into the city to St Patrick's Cathedral, we sang the words of the Robin Mark song that was rapidly becoming the anthem for our walk:

   **"Shout to the North and the South,
   Sing to the East and the West,
   Jesus is Saviour to all;
    Lord of heaven and earth."**

We were greeted in Armagh city by many of our church family and together we prayed

and praised before heading home for a longer and much warmer bath for the feet than they were able to have in the street fountain in Clones!

CROSS WALK LEG 1:
Ballyconnel Beach, Sligo to Navan fort, Armagh | 105 miles

A Short Interlude

In the week immediately following Leg 1, I travelled with our family across the Irish Sea to Oxford where, on 2nd July, I had the privilege of marrying my oldest son Chris to his fiancée Suzy in Abingdon Methodist Church.

Both of them wanted a no fuss wedding with a simple service of praise, a party picnic in the park and an opportunity to play games of touch rugby and Frisbee and take a swim in a weir in the river.

Chris's Granda Martin was there and, on one of the most glorious days of the summer, fell asleep in the Park. When he woke some time later he was heard to remark, "That was one of the best wedding receptions I have ever been to!"

It was relaxed and stress free throughout. Chris and Suzy's idea of 'The Best Wedding Picture of All Time' was a time lapse taken by one of their guests. I leave it to you to decide whether a more conventional pose of bride and groom with well attired family additions would have been more to your liking. Normally it is considered to be the bride's day, but even she didn't make the cut!

I give you the groom (3rd from the right) and his mates...

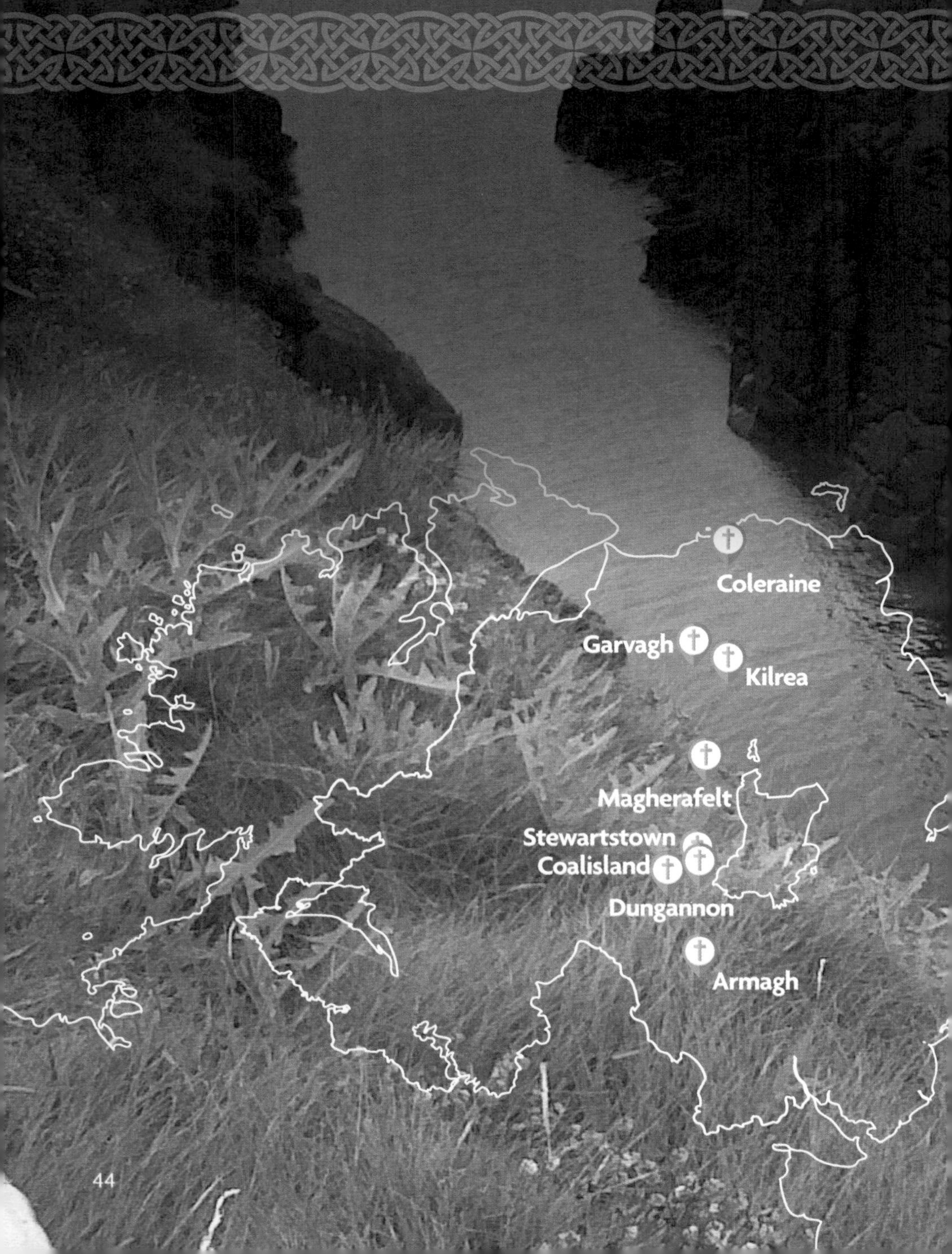

Coleraine

Garvagh

Kilrea

Magherafelt

Stewartstown
Coalisland

Dungannon

Armagh

A Walk from the North

CROSS WALK LEG 2
Portrush to Armagh

CROSS WALK LEG 2
Portrush to Armagh

This leg of the journey was the only one where we didn't head directly to the coast to camp. The plan was to park the caravan up and stay overnight at the point we were walking to the next day.

Keith Dundas was the original contact that led to this overnight stop point. Over six weeks earlier he had visited Richhill Elim. I bumped into him in the T Junction (our church café and social area). I asked where he was living and when he said near Kilrea, I told him that we just might need a bed in July in Kilrea! He asked why on earth I needed a bed and so Andy Magwood and I outlined the vision for the Cross Walk. The following Saturday he rang us to say that he had spoken with the Minister of Churchtown Presbyterian Church, where he and his wife Donna attended and were involved as youth leaders.

What Keith shared from his conversation with his Minister was interesting...

- The name and theme of their Holiday Bible Week that year was 'Cross Purposes'.
- It was traditionally held in August - but not this year. For the first time, it was being held in July.
- Their Minister had prepared only four of the five epilogues he was scheduled to deliver.

Despite his best efforts, he was stuck for one night - his Tuesday night talk. Even though he didn't know it then, Keith's Minister was later going to learn that his attendance would be required at another meeting that hadn't, at this stage, been arranged.

When he had heard of our proposed visit, he asked Keith to find out which night we were likely to be passing through Kilrea. Oddly enough, it was that very same Tuesday night and so our first official speaking engagement was arranged before the walk even embarked from Richhill.

WEDNESDAY 22ND JUNE

Getting started out on the shortest leg of the Cross Walk seemed to get more complicated as the day progressed for our worship leader, Andy Magwood. My plane was delayed on its return from England, so I had to connect en route with Andy. The first minute together inside the pickup saw Andy's satellite navigation system break down and refuse to do anything! After praying, it sparked back into life and it was all systems go. This, however, was only the first of several technical glitches, including frozen mobile phones and unrecognizable postcodes. That said, it is probably not surprising given that we were trying to find a place called Tamlaght O'Crilly! I think we might have been better off using the more culturally proficient 'Jon Joe' satellite navigation system, manufactured in Ireland, by Irish men for use on Irish roads!

After much prayer and a late drive, we arrived in the grounds beside the local Presbyterian manse where the Holiday Bible Week club was being held. Keith was there to greet us when we eventually got there. He parked us up beside an out-building that would make a

wonderful barn conversion/holiday home if it had been located in France. Exploration of the site showed a sizeable marquee had been erected for the event which, over the week, would host two groups; the 7.00pm slot for primary school children and the 9.00pm slot for secondary school children. After we had set up the caravan for the night, we were invited by Keith and Donna for supper which we thoroughly enjoyed and then retired to the caravan, only for Andy to be kept awake for most of the night by what he described as "an owl with a chest cold and throat infection, snoring through a megaphone!" Poor Andy! Meanwhile, I slept.

With one of us well rested, we set out to the church's early morning prayer meeting at 7am. We were made very welcome indeed and enjoyed praying with a room full of people eager to give glory to God for the previous evening at the Holiday Bible Week. We also lifted the ensuing evening before God and requested His help.

E

We then left and drove to Ramore Head, Portrush, to the point due North from Armagh.

As the walk was about to begin from the Atlantic Ocean, I spotted a motionless seagull sitting right beside the water's edge. As I walked over to it and stroked its back, I thought of the song lyrics we sometimes sang 'Rise up oh church with broken wings'. I was considering picking it up to encourage it to fly from the awkward spot in which it lay but I sensed danger and had a distinct impression not to lift it nor go back near it. I don't know if they bite, but I wasn't about to give it a hand to nibble on! It felt like a warning to be careful.

We left Portrush for the very, very wet pull up the road to Coleraine and stopped off to pray at Ballywillan Presbyterian Church. I was standing like a drowned rat when a lovely wee lady came past with a cup of coffee in each hand and thanked me for praying.

In Coleraine town centre (and soaked again) we prayed beside the town hall, with its weather vane on top depicting North, South, East and West.

Afterwards, we decided that a long overdue coffee would be very welcome. Andy asked the first couple coming round the corner where we could go to find a coffee shop. Without asking too many questions they directed us to a nearby coffee shop and offered to pay for our coffee that morning. What a blessing they were to us.

The couple had just dropped their children off to the Scripture Union Missions Camp,

CSSM. We talked intently for over an hour, until I was concerned that they would get a parking ticket! Together we left the coffee shop and went to a Christian Youth Project. They kindly offered us a room where we spent two and a half hours with the couple. They had a heart to serve God, but issues of criticism in the church had dampened their enthusiasm for outreach into one of the local estates. **The enemy of our souls will always attempt to steal joy and our enthusiasm if we let him!** With them, he had all but succeeded. The gentleman had been a builder of blocks, but the prospect of working with prickly people and building them back together was appearing less and less appealing! **By the time we came to pray with them they both knew they had had a God encounter and had opened themselves up to the probability of a call of God on their lives that needed to be seriously addressed by both of them. This they were willing to investigate with open hearts and renewed enthusiasm.**

Back on our walk, as we pulled up the hill after crossing the Lower Bann River we met an 82 year old man, whom I now refer to as Danny boy. He sang to us at the roadside a song with incredible God centred lyrics that, I think he said, he had written himself. It was one of the most wonderful moments of the day. I could feel the hair standing on the back of my neck as I watched this old man being so mightily used in the ministry of two soaked-through travellers.

We needed to capture this magical moment, so Andy used the pick-up cab as an impromptu recording studio and an iPhone as the sound desk.

Danny boy sang his lyrics to the tune of the famous Irish folk ballad set during the Great Irish Famine, 'The Fields of Athenry':

I believe that Jesus died and
gave his life for you and me
He shed his love that we may all be free
He broke the prison walls so
that we might hear his call
Now (inaudible) for you and for me.

Glory to God who reigns on high
Renew me now for this is my heart's cry
Your love O Lord I sing; I praise you as my King
Come fill me Holy Spirit from on high.

No more loneliness, His
presence is here for you and me
He shed His love that we may all be free
The glory overcame; at His
knee we will bow down
As we hold our head up high, with dignity.

Glory to God who reigns on high
Renew me now for this is my heart's cry
Your love O Lord I sing; I praise you as my King
Come fill me Holy Spirit from on high.

On probably the first record Danny boy ever cut, we caught most of the song, with the exception of one unclear line. We thanked him and parted company, him blessing us much, much more than we could him.

The rest of the afternoon saw us pushing South. With only two on the team, the time on the road was longer and the rests shorter but still the miles and the God moments continued to encourage us. Claire, who had been working up North that day, arrived again, as she had done the previous Tuesday, to cook tea for us and encourage us for a short time. Thanks to that, we actually had 20 minutes to gobble it down and prepare some thoughts for the young people's meeting. As I prayed, I sensed the Holy Spirit telling me to share with them about my son Ben and 'the trailer incident'.

So in the meeting I told them this story...

Our second son Ben, who was 10 years old at the time, was helping me with a trailer load of stones. We were helping Rosemary Graham, a widow, to do some work around her house. She was just another forgotten statistic in the long Troubles that impacted our land. The first night I met Rosemary, she was sitting in the kitchen crying - some several years after her husband had been shot dead in Lurgan. The Holy Spirit simply indicated that I had to help in this house. And so began what was almost a six month project for the church: all of the trees that were overgrown around the house were removed and the garden re-fenced. We painted the exterior of the house and attempted to leave the garden as maintenance free as possible.

On the final night of the project, I was bringing in 1.5 metric tons of red ornamental stones to complete the borders. Upon arriving at the entrance to the house, Ben stepped off the front of the trailer to remove a cone and unknown to me I had run over the top of him and crushed him vertically underneath the twin axle trailer. I shall never forget looking under that trailer. It was a scene of complete horror. By the time we got the trailer removed from off the top of him, I watched his blood reddening the Ballygroobaney Road. I had no idea if he would live or die or if he would ever walk again. I got down on my knees, dressed in a boiler suit, and immediately prayed over him. The woman we were working for was a nurse and she knew we were in serious trouble. He was rushed on a spine board to the Royal Victoria Hospital in Belfast where he was examined by one of the top trauma and orthopaedic surgeons, Niall Eames (the son of the then Primate).

After his initial assessment of Ben, Mr Eames told me that my son had sustained "an horrific injury" and the terminology he used was that "his spinal cord was exposed as if in the middle of broken glass", such was the significant damage done to the spinal column. The operation was considered so tricky and delicate that he did not want to begin it during the night watch. Despite still being dressed in the boiler-suit, I told him I was a Christian and that our church and family would be praying for him and his team when they felt it was time to begin.

A long night of waiting began, only to be followed by an even longer day of waiting as a full surgical team spent all of the following day attempting a spinal fusion. At 8:15pm the following evening, in the Intensive Care Unit for Sick Children, Mr Eames told me that no-one that he had operated on, with injuries as extensive as Ben's, had ever walked again. I felt for him and his team as he must have been working under ferocious strain with a 100% failure rate up to that point.

As for us as parents? Hearing those words from the expert were very hard to hear. Around that time in our lives, an African Pastor had been invited to speak at our church in Richhill. When I gave him the pulpit he set his notes down, indicating that that was what he had planned to say, but that had just been changed! He then pointed at me and, as if it were yesterday, I remember him saying, "You are God's man and you must speak life into situations where you see death and hope into situations where you see hopelessness." This was one of those moments. We chose to speak out life. We chose to believe for life. We could do none other.

After only eight days and without a single painkiller ever in his mouth, Ben got up and walked out of the Royal Victoria Hospital! He went on to study Sports Science at The University of Ulster, Jordanstown and has been playing rugby and other high impact *sports and is now an athletics director at a Christian Mission School in Wuhan in China. We are so grateful to our God and to the surgeon and his team for their skill and the incredible outcome.*

On the Sunday evening when I returned to Richhill having spent eight full days in the Royal Victoria Hospital, I told the incredible story of God's intervention and how, as a father, I had looked at my own son's blood covering the road and the impact that had on me. That said, I still had no idea or conception of what God the Father must have felt when he saw His son Jesus shedding his blood for the sins of men and women. After the service, in the (recently constructed) coffee shop adjoining Richhill Elim, the girl whom God had sent to us as a baker declared her trust in Christ as Lord of her life. Every strategic move we took to develop the site in Richhill has been met with significant opposition. I've seen three of my four children at death's door since the call into the ministry. Opposition in the spiritual realm is all too real. You don't need to experience it to believe it. Believe it!

Having shared the story of Ben and his accident, we finished the night in the Holiday Bible club, singing our anthem song 'Shout to the North and the South...' We wanted the children to do the actions and turn to the four compass points as they sang. Before we began, I asked a local to identify due north. He did and off we set. The only problem was that this eejit from Armagh still at the front and directing things got confused between East and West, causing much confusion and merriment to all. Chaos apart, the night

had been a good one. We packed up and chatted with the minister (who had arrived later in the meeting) and I asked if he had enjoyed the end of the meeting. He replied with demure humour, "Well, at least I didn't hear you preach any heresy." I suppose from a Presbyterian minister, one would have to consider that a compliment!

We had supper again with Keith and Donna Dundas. At one point, after midnight, Keith looked at his wife and asked, "Well, are you going to ask or will I?" A long silence ensued and Donna started to fill up with tears. They said, "We haven't really talked this through with many people but we have been trying for a baby and have been told by the doctors that we are unable to unless we consider a certain type of treatment." They had an appointment in two days' time with a consultant.

I asked what the issue was. Donna relayed the story of how she too had had a trailer accident as a young girl, which meant she may not be able to conceive a child naturally. As a young woman, she slowly processed the enormity of having her long term hope of being a mother altered forever by the accident. She eventually came to terms with that devastating news. When she met Keith and realised there was chance he might be her husband, she told him that if they married there may be no young Dundas children. He would need to be prepared to walk that path if the relationship was to develop further. Keith believed Donna was the girl for him and told her that hers was the only journey he wanted to be a part of!

53

Some significant time after, they were finally married on the 28th July 2006. After trying for a number of years to have children, they were referred to infertility specialists for tests, only to discover the ultimate irony that the possible issue lay with Keith and not Donna. With this knowledge, the medical profession offered potential help in a form of IVF treatment called ICSI. It is very hard to imagine the highs and lows of the rollercoaster of emotions this young couple were being forced to face.

They asked me to pray for them and, in particular, for their consultation on the Thursday of that week. I felt that I couldn't and said, "No, I can't". I asked them to let me walk with the cross the following day and I promised to return to their house and share with them anything that God impressed upon me about their situation. We said goodnight and I knew as we were leaving that they were very disappointed that I had felt I couldn't pray. I too was puzzled by the fact I had said such an emphatic "No!" and so quickly too. It had clearly stung, given that they had not shared with any strangers their personal plight. Andy and I went back to the caravan.

TUESDAY 5TH JULY

During the night I awoke about 3.45am with an overwhelming compulsion to go to the toilet. I climbed out of the sleeping bag and made my way to the portaloo at the top of the hill beside the marquee, only to discover that the need had gone! Very odd indeed given that the compulsion had woken me from sleep.

So, I stepped outside and stopped for a while to listen for Andy's owl with a chest cold and throat infection, snoring through a megaphone. I have to admit, his sanity was indeed confirmed at the sound of a mighty beastie and its snore! As I stood listening to it, I was aware of being beneath a very cloudy sky and, as it was a balmy night, I stood outside and then watched the growing light. As I did, I felt I should go into the marquee to pray. This I did and began praying for their Bible Week. As I prayed more, I felt a very clear direction from the Holy Spirit to lift the Bible at the front and read the story of Abraham and Sarah. I was aware of being asked a very precise question: Where were they when they received the promise?

Sarah, I knew, had laughed from within the inner tent, but I did not recall exactly where Abram was when he too had received the promise. As I hunted through the Scriptures, I discovered the part where Abram had been given his promise in Genesis 15: 4-5 "And behold, the word of the Lord came to him, saying, 'This one shall not be your heir,' but one who will come from your own body shall be your heir.' Then He brought him outside and said, 'Look now toward heaven, and count the stars if you are able to number them'.

And He said to him, so shall your descendants be.'" (NKJV).

So, for the first time, I realised that both of them had been inside the tent when they received the promise. I thought about this and the implications of restricted living conditions and restricted views. So often tents limit our thinking and can stop us believing and expecting a God (who is bigger than the universe) to open His possibilities to our finite minds and lives. Even as a tent can restrict our perspective at a natural level, so too various things like words and restrictive viewpoints or man decreed, self-constructed doctrines can limit our spiritual vision.

I felt God reiterate those same thoughts to me... Clive step outside... my heart was beating faster as I did. **Stepping outside the tent, there in the south sky was one single bright shining star** (from my previous horlicks of the song when I confused east and west, I learnt that at least I knew my north and south!) Unlike the wise men from the east, I was an Irishman from the west and didn't know much about the overhead constellations at all - was it a bright north star? If so, what was it doing in the south sky? I had no idea about the mechanics overhead, but I did know Almighty God was speaking. As I looked up at the star, I prayed. Was God about to turn this young couple's life the right way up? As I returned to the caravan to try and catch some sleep the words of the chorus of an old hymn came to me,

At the cross, at the cross, where I first saw the light and the burden of my heart rolled away. It was there by faith I received my sight And now I am happy all the day! (Isaac Watts, 1707)

The time I had noticed the star was 4:30am. I tried to sleep but I couldn't. The thoughts and wonderings whether there was anything too hard for God and of course the wittering of a beastie with a sore throat prevailed!

Again, as we had done the previous morning, we joined the church at 7am for their prayer meeting and Keith and Donna afterwards, for breakfast. I shared with them that I did not want to add to their roller-coaster of emotions but outlined what had happened to me through the night hours. I told them of the visit of that African pastor during the early part of my ministry in Richhill, and of his deeply embedded two line sermon etched in my mind. I told them I never forgot that night and have ever after tried to believe for and fight for life and hope at every conceivable opportunity. This morning, in this home, amid tears and so mindful of their bruised and battered hearts, we prayed. We prayed for

both of them but specifically for Donna to be healed and receive the gift of the child they so longed for. As I left, I did not realise at the time that Keith and Donna felt confused by my prayer as they believed the problem lay with Keith.

The next day they were to go and see their consultant who told them that something had showed up on Donna's latest test which ruled out IVF and they should go home and think about adoption as there would never be a young Dundas baby in their home.

The Doctors had spoken; let God arise!

It would be some 13 weeks before we learned what happened. When next they travelled to Richhill to see Andy and I, they brought a 12 week scan picture of their new wee baby! Donna was pregnant, a double infertility miracle. I kept recalling the words that we had preached in Uganda,

"Is there anything too hard for the Lord?"

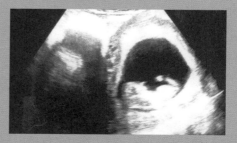

WEDNESDAY 6TH JULY

The next morning's walk started in Garvagh with prayer at the clock tower, rain lashing down our necks. Some very hard yards awaited us that day. It was a morning again of "just doing it", though that particular part of the walk was brightened significantly with the receipt of some lovely texts about the impact of the meeting the previous night.

We stopped for lunch in a place called the Country Cafe. Towards the end of our meal an unusually dressed guy paced the cafe wall-to-wall. His activity was bizarre and we noted that, of about 12-15 customers, we were the only two being cordoned off behind an invisible line he was walking backward and forwards along. Andy went to the bathroom and, whilst there, prayed. He sensed that witchcraft was being used specifically against us. We paid our bill and, as Andy left to continue walking with the cross, I sat in the pick-up wondering whether to engage or not with our unusual stranger. It was then that I received a phone call from a Pastor in Portadown. He asked exactly what was going on right there and right then. I asked why he was interested. He said, "For some reason I have felt led to pray for your protection and have been marching up and down from one end of my office to the other, wall to wall, praying for you two men. Are you ok?" I thanked him a lot for his prayers and his sensitivity to the Spirit. I recalled the warning, right at the outset of this leg, with the unusual gull at the water's edge and the warning not to lift it.

The day brightened with some good conversations on the road as we headed for Magherafelt. Two encounters that afternoon bemused me somewhat. Two people stopped with me and attempted to show me the way of salvation, wrongly assuming that this was some sort of pilgrimage that accomplished salvation by works. The first one who arrived was dressed in a Manchester United football top (so I could tell that he had little discernment in the spiritual realm and a lot less in the natural realm!). The second, Hazel, tried to ensure I was truly a Christian. She had been a backslider but in the previous four months God had been working very clearly in her life again. She told me that she and her husband had been discussing the possibility of doing something of a positive spiritual nature in Co. Kildare. She had no clear idea of what form that service might take and so I offered her the opportunity to accompany us on the southern leg of the Cross Walk. The suddenness of the offer to land her there, and so soon, left her lost for words. She had tried to rescue me but our God had turned the tables on her with an unexpected offer to launch their new ministry. I suspect she left thinking about how often we think we are ahead of God when in truth, we will always come second in the race to know the future, even if it is our own! It would be great to see a couple more full-time missionaries serving in the harvest fields in Kildare when God knows they are ready.

As a result of these two bemusing but lengthy engagements, we terminated that night somewhat shy of our planned finish in the town of Magherafelt and drove in to

meet some of the leaders of The Lighthouse Fellowship who run an outreach project to share the love of God with the younger generation of the area. Andy and his group 'Inflame' had sung at their Saturday and Sunday night meetings many times over recent years. Though they were all new faces to me, Andy's friends soon felt like old friends to me too as we shared warm fellowship together at the buildings where they hold their meetings.

In town that night we met seven people who had two things in common - a love for the Lord and a love for the young people in their community. We explained our vision to The Lighthouse leaders like Leslie Barfoot and Andy Campbell, and that we were here to pray in the centre of their town for a blessing in their community.

Paul, the owner of a local coffee shop, was a little nervous about the public nature of our witness. He asked, "Clive, are you seriously asking me to get down on my knees beneath a 12 foot cross and pray Isaiah 45:8 in the

Diamond with all of my customers driving past?" I answered, "I'm not here to force anyone to do anything but I know God has called me to do this in your town." Over a cup of coffee, we shared some of the extraordinary encounters we had had on Leg 1 of the Cross Walk. Paul in particular seemed enthralled and declared that he was going to nail his colours to the mast! To his credit, he came out with the group and hunkered down on his hands and knees and prayed for his town.

After we had prayed I gave him one of our cards and encouraged him to pray the words of the two verses on the floor of his business premises in the morning, before either his staff or customers arrived for work or coffee. He promised to do exactly that.

Having completed our work that day we were driven out to a beautiful log cabin at a lake on Leslie's father's farm.

It was a glorious evening and we shared testimonies, late into the night, of the power of the living God. It was the first time I had shared my life story in a very long time.

THURSDAY 7TH JULY

We started a little later than usual owing to the fact that I had spent the morning talking to Willie Barfoot. He recounted how, some 40 years earlier, he had kneeled down in a ploughed field and asked the Lord Jesus Christ into his life. It was a decision that was to affect the rest of his life. I love the old saints; I love their stories. Jesus Christ, as the Bible says, is indeed the same yesterday, today and forever and is still in the same business of rescuing lives from every era.

Our logistics manager, Alan, re-joined us from a short visit to Scotland where he had been to graduate from his theological studies. It was great to see him again and even better to see the stuffed bacon rolls he arrived with, which were a terrific treat! **We three resumed our walk with more rain, more rain and even more rain.**

At 2pm that afternoon there had been a radio interview booked for us with UCB Ireland radio. We were given a great opportunity to explain the Cross Walk journey and our rationale. However, during the interview, the phone line to the studio dropped five or six times and Alex, the presenter, was becoming frustrated. The studio manager asked what on earth was going on with us. We explained that we were sitting in the middle of a massive thunder and lightning storm which seemed to be directly overhead. He persevered one more time until I had shared our two key verses we wanted their listeners to hear - Isaiah 45:8 and Jeremiah 22:29. I would like to thank UCB technical staff and Alex in particular, for their perseverance that day because, as we were about to find out, it

was just at the time another God moment was beginning to unfold.

That afternoon, all the lights went out in both Cookstown and Magherafelt with the notable exception of Paul's coffee shop! Paul drove south to Stewartstown later that evening to catch up with us and eagerly relayed the strange goings on that day. Many people had come into his shop that afternoon and asked him, "How come you're the only man in Magherafelt with light this afternoon?" As Andy said later in good old Northern Irish vernacular, "Clive, he was more lit than his shop!" I laughed at his turn of phrase. For Paul, I think this may have been a lesson in always putting God first, regardless of what other people might think.

Several weeks after that afternoon, a visitor to Richhill Elim Church explained that on the day that the interview was conducted, he had been driving eastward from Donegal. He had seen the lightning storm and told me that it was one of the most unusual lightning strikes that he had ever seen.

Paul, during the same journey, delivered a CD to the team with the message "Pastor Clive will need to hear this." It was a recording of a lecture given by Margaret Keogh, a prayer intercessor for Ireland. It was to provide a fascinating bedtime story that night as we settled down to rest in the caravan.

She unveiled many fascinating insights into her research and intercession concerning the spiritual history of our nation. She made mention of Irish poet, W.B. Yeats and other literary and legal contributors such as Patrick Pearse, a teacher, barrister, writer and one of the leaders of the 1916 Easter Rising. Their writings occasionally referred to a fascination with some of the goddesses in Irish mythology like Eire, the goddess of war and the three separate phases of her existence. The story goes that when Eire had arrived in the last old woman phase of her existence, her rejuvenation back to a young goddess would demand the blood of young Irish men to be spilled on the land. Patrick Pearse makes mention of this concept in his writings on arms and war when he attaches an unusual degree of importance to the notion of blood sacrifice. He desired martyrdom to

try to ensure the immortality and redemption of his people and wrote, "bloodshed is a cleansing and a sanctifying thing and a nation which regards it as the final horror has lost its manhood" (www.qub.ac.uk/sites/irishhistorylive).

Of particular interest to us at this particular point on our journey was some of the information that she had shared with regard to Navan Fort. Keogh described its history as a scene of pagan worship and religion. At one stage it had been ritualistically closed down and sealed. Without explaining that process in any detail, she referred to the fact that, in the mid-1960s, an archaeology team from Queen's University in Belfast had re-opened the site. This, she argued, contributed in the spiritual realm to the aftermath of the next 30 years 'Troubles', when thousands of young men lost their lives in the struggle for political power. She may be right, in my opinion, and if her analysis is accurate it may indeed point to Navan Fort as being a site with spiritual significance. She also made mention of the fact that, during the early period of the Troubles, paramilitary organisations used to light fires on top of it in order to "draw power" from the site and receive the benefit of its dark and hidden forces.

As the lecture explored in much more depth the history surrounding both literary and political thinkers on the island, I was struck that the Holy Spirit had confirmed that our walks from each of the four shorelines should indeed culminate and unite over the top of Navan Fort.

Indeed, many centuries earlier, had St. Patrick not walked from Strangford headed for that very same location? As with so many other aspects of the Cross Walk, we felt again as if we had been handed another jigsaw puzzle piece in a picture that God was forming in our nation at this time.

We had unusual guardians that night - two brown Labradors who assigned themselves as watchdogs. Despite the fact they must have had a warm bed nearby, they chose instead to sleep outside our caravan door in what were atrocious conditions. Camped beside the forest, it felt good to have them nearby; at least at one stage of the night their services seemed to have been needed, given the racket they were to raise in our defence!

FRIDAY 8TH JULY

We journeyed through Coalisland (where Alan met old friends who had been close to him when he had worked there) and on to Dungannon where we had lunch, courtesy of the Vineyard Church. We visited The Storehouse (their project to help provide essentials and practical help and support to people and families in need) and prayed together with them in the office, sensing a tremendous sense of peace as we did.

Passing Donnelly's Motorstore on the outskirts of Dungannon, we attempted to trade a single-wheeled vehicle for anything with four wheels but it proved unsuccessful (and unsurprising). Raymond Donnelly has, in the past, been generous to us as a family on many occasions but today was not one of them!

This compass was on the floor of the car showroom - very appropriate!

The journey to Navan Fort that afternoon was walked in bright sunshine.

Unofficial stops at homes along the way, including that of good Samaritans Helen and Patrick, helped replenish tired legs.

We made it back to the centre of Armagh for a late tea and some more of Mrs Joy Glass' scones - they were worth the walk alone had nothing else been achieved! Thanks to all who provided food and drinks along the way - many, many thanks.

CROSS WALK LEG 2:
Portrush to Armagh City | 73 miles

Following in the steps of St. Patrick

CROSS WALK LEG 3
Strangford to Armagh

Strangford
ugh
llan

CROSS WALK LEG 3
Strangford to Armagh

MONDAY 18TH JULY

An hour before I left home, a phone call came in from one of our contacts Mr Leslie Gray - he had provided hospitality for us on Leg 1 of the Cross Walk. He posed a question: "Clive, have you read those prophecies I gave you?" Somewhat puzzled, I enquired which prophecies he was referring to, as this was the first I had heard of them. He indicated that he had given them to Alan. Later that day, when we met up as a team, one of the first questions I posed to Alan was regarding the whereabouts of the aforementioned prophecies and why I had never heard of them. His defence was that he was holding them in safe keeping for a time when things slowed down a little for me - a month on, still not a minute!

We drove over the Co. Down drumlins to Strangford and camped at the quayside that night, beside The Narrows of Strangford Lough, one of the largest sea inlets in the UK.

TUESDAY 19TH JULY

The following morning we started off again on foot from the Irish Sea and I walked the few hundred metres into the centre of Strangford village to pray the words of Isaiah 45:8 in the centre.

When I got back onto my feet after praying in the centre of Strangford, my legs felt like lead and the cross so much heavier than at anytime before. It was easily the toughest half mile stint in the entire Cross Walk journey of 430 miles. I suspected there was more to it than the fact I was out of condition from the lack of walking in the previous week when my daughter had graduated from university in Newcastle Upon Tyne.

I was glad to hand the cross over and get seated down in the jeep to catch my breath. I reached over and picked up the assortment of some nine prophecies in total from various intercessors in different parts of the world

who had been praying about Ireland. The very first one I read was received in the exact location that I currently found myself. It was a timely read:

In the summer of 1997, I returned to my childhood hobby of sea fishing, largely because my normal water-sports of dinghy sailing and water-skiing were impractical because of a cracked rib. On Saturday 2nd August, two friends and I headed out through the strong current of the Strangford Narrows and over the often turbulent bar mouth which, on this particular day, was as calm as a mill pond. We drifted out to sea with the last run of the outgoing tide and began fishing about a mile offshore. As we settled down to a quiet afternoon's jigging, the silence was gently broken by a soft hissing, blowing sound. We looked around amazed to see that we were surrounded by a small school of porpoises. I was excited because, in over 30 years of water-sports in and around Northern Irish waters, I had never seen these beautiful animals. Slightly smaller than dolphins, they roam the world's oceans following, by sophisticated sonar, shoals of fish on which they feed. The water temperature was abnormally warm this year and this factor, combined with the abundant fish stocks, had attracted them here. Almost immediately, we began to catch fish. We had expected to catch mackerel but instead we caught mostly cod, sometimes three or four at a time. It was such a catch from the Irish Sea that I had not seen in a very long time. As we looked and hollered "I'm in!" time after time, we watched the porpoises circling and feeding as we both

enjoyed a rich harvest.

I began to reflect on how different our present experience was from the troubled image of Northern Ireland that so often flashes around the world. It was then that I felt God speaking to me in my spirit saying that he was going to ask me to prophesy a blessing. Most of the other prophecies that I had been given included a large element of "Repent ye!" Now God was asking me whether I would like to prophesy blessing? The question challenged my negative man-centred fixation with the Northern Irish 'Troubles' and reminded me that this beautiful land which I love was God's land and He has his own purposes for it. I waited for the messages of blessing to come...

It would be several weeks later when I was involved in an extended time of worship during a service in Christian Fellowship Church, Belfast, that I felt God give this interpretation of our experience with the porpoises.

Just as the porpoises had travelled thousands of miles to feed on the rich harvest in the Irish Sea, so people would come from all over the world to feed at the rich harvest that God was preparing here in Ireland.

Experienced right **here** at the Strangford Narrows where I was right **now**. How extraordinary? God's timing is ALWAYS perfect. I sat somewhat stunned by what I had just read. That feeling was about to be added to...

What Leslie Gray had provided proved intriguing. Again, as with the CD that we had been presented with on Leg 2 of the Cross Walk which provided some unique insights into the past at Navan Fort, here too it appeared that God was providing more jigsaw puzzle pieces which pointed to the future.

The second example of prophecy about Ireland that I began to absorb was a contribution from Dennis Cramer dated back to 1997:

Supernatural Peace

God's promise for Ireland is that all things will become new. She will have a fresh start like that of springtime. God will stamp newness and freshness all over Ireland and Northern Ireland. Such will be the magnificent release of His love to them. Love, forgiveness, healing, and reconciliation will flow in this land. Ireland will have one people, one government, one economy, one currency, one goal, one future. All will become as it was meant to be. The devil will go down in defeat, and mighty angels will be flying back and forth over Ireland and Northern Ireland, crying, "Peace, peace, peace!" And there will be peace; supernatural peace, permanent peace, the peace that surpasses all human understanding. Somehow - supernaturally, sovereign, mysteriously, and suddenly - all the internal feuding will end. The unprecedented ceasing of old hostilities will announce the arrival of the Prince of Peace. None other than the Prince of Life, Jesus Christ Himself, will arrive to visit this formerly troubled land,

bringing lasting peace where there has been no peace.

An Army of Young Evangelists

Consequently, a massive revival among Ireland's very young people will take place. This sudden outbreak of Holy Spirit revival fire will cover the land, even affecting Scotland. A second target group, slightly older than the first, the 20 to 30 year-old group, will also see a tremendous move of God. Married couples will flood into churches in huge numbers as God redeems their hearts. They will cease from their pursuit of material things and run hard after spiritual things. Many missionaries will emerge from this move of God. With their original destiny in God realized, many converts - single and married - will join the army of evangelists that God will raise up. They will take the gospel to many lands.

Another mile down the road it was my turn to carry the cross again. I was so intrigued, though, by what I had read that I found it difficult to drag myself out of the pickup and do my fair share. Whilst the team were often gracious, they were no fools either, so out I had to get out and walk! The rest would have to wait...

As I started out on my second lift that day, my heart was lighter and my legs fresher. I began to reflect on all the hard walks over the previous two legs. Midsummer's day in particular was horrendously difficult given the rainfall we tramped through. We also experienced days like that one on Leg 2, with thunder and lightning directly overhead to boot... rain, rain and more rain!

Now, however, in a matter of minutes after reading those first couple of prophecies that had been released over our nation, I started to see things a whole lot differently, particularly concerning those long 'soaked-to-the-skin' days. I reflected on Isaiah 45:8, the verse that I had felt strongly the Holy Spirit required us to pray on our journey, that 'the heavens would rain righteousness.' Could it just be possible that Cramer's prophecy was being fulfilled as literally in the physical realm as we believed it would be in the spiritual realm?

Not that far away from the Eastern shoreline we had just left behind, during the revival in the Hebrides between 1949 and 1952, two elderly sisters, housebound and infirm, were unable to attend church but made their small home a prayer closet. Peggy and Christine Smith, both in their 80s and weak in flesh, one blind and the other crippled with arthritis, became mighty intercessors and friends of God. The Lord gave them the promise of Isaiah 44:3.

"For I will pour water upon him that is thirsty, and floods upon the dry ground: I will pour my spirit upon thy seed, and my blessing upon thine offspring." (KJV)

They contended for this promise and for their island in prayer day and night.

Is Ireland the same? Are people thirsty or couldn't we care? Is our land dry and aware of its need of refreshing floods from our Heavenly Father?

PONDERING ON ST. PATRICK

This I did as I headed for Downpatrick. Although we have very few written records with which to shed light on the life of St Patrick, the most famous passage in Confessio, his autobiography, tells of a dream after his return to Britain in which he is delivered a letter headed, "The Voice of the Irish."

'I saw a man coming, as it were from Ireland. His name was Victoricus, and he carried many letters, and he gave me one of them. I read the heading: "The Voice of the Irish". As I began the letter, I imagined in that moment that I heard the voice of those very people who were near the wood of Foclut, which is beside the western sea—and they cried out, as with one voice: "We appeal to you, holy servant boy, to come and walk among us."'

My thoughts centred on what Patrick must have felt, walking this same way, hearing the call of the Irish, 'to come and walk among us.' When he did, he was heading towards Ireland's oldest city, Armagh. The then ancient capital of Ulster was the birthplace of Brian Boru, the last High King of Ireland. One of the Royal sites of Ireland, Navan

Fort was home to the High Kings of Ulster in ancient times and it is for this reason that historians think Patrick selected Armagh as his principal centre in Ireland. St Patrick's Church of Ireland is one of the most ancient Christian sites in Ireland and has a direct line back to St Patrick's involvement in the church in 455AD. It is also the burial place of Brian Boru.

As I was lost centuries back in time in my thinking, a cyclist rode past me, only to double back and engage me. His turning back was the first time that I was consciously aware of such a pattern of behaviour but it was to become a trend that was to repeat itself many, many times over the Cross Walk. It was that day that I became aware that the compulsion to do a u-turn was somehow significant.

The cyclist turned out to be an unemployed plasterer, of which there were many due to the downturn in the building industry in Ireland. Since he had been made redundant, he kept fit by cycling five times a week around the same route, and had done for the previous couple of years.

Today, oddly for him, he had decided to take an alternative route, stopping to talk to me at length about the deep spiritual questions that had been brooding on his mind.

Every few minutes the conversation was punctuated with a look of amazement and him saying... "But I NEVER, EVER come this way!"

He had had melanoma concerns a couple of years prior and had, as a result of that and his work slowing down, been thinking a lot about the meaning of life. By the time an hour had passed we prayed and he seemed to know that he had had a God encounter.

They say you need to know what you are going to do in life by the time you are 40 (I made it by just a couple of months!) and he too was now almost 40 years of age. He reminded me of myself years ago, chasing the pound note too hard. He also reminded me of the Scribe in the Bible who came asking a key question of Jesus. When the discussion was concluded, Jesus said to him "You are not far from the Kingdom of God" (Mark 12:34, NKJV).

I prayed his journey into the Kingdom would be completed soon, very soon.

We kept heading for Downpatrick and spent some time at the new £6.3m St Patrick's visitor centre built beside Down Cathedral; then we left Patrick to the tourists and walked on.

In the afternoon as we journeyed through Clough we noticed that the man in the life-sized cow and farmer sculpture in the centre of the roundabout was sporting a freshly adorned sash - no doubt the work of local pranksters over the recent Twelfth of July celebrations. We eventually made it up the big hill into Castlewellan where many intrigued enquirers stopped to question what exactly we were up to. We spoke with Catherine and her friend (two teenage girls) who asked some very searching questions as to how God speaks and guides an individual on their journey through life. Several other folks were drawn into the conversation affording us the opportunity to pray with them for their town.

We made it a few miles beyond Castlewellan before we eventually decided to call it a day and drove to our next port of call. That evening we were to have an evening with author Mike Oman at the old Youth With A Mission (YWAM) centre in Closkelt.

The setting and the view from our high vantage point of the surrounding Mourne Mountains was wonderful and the best thing about it all was the fact that the burgers were already well cooked on the barbecue (thank you Alan). We spent a great night of fellowship with Mike and Roz Oman and their daughter.

Before we were due to retire for the night, we decided to have a time of prayer together. During that time of waiting upon God, Mike had a picture impressed upon his mind of our Cross Walk Team like the "bow of a ship pushing through a viscous atmosphere." As he watched it the thick, sticky atmosphere, between a solid and liquid, was parted and the unusual thing about it was the fact that it did not close back in on itself after the cross had passed through it but remained in the open state.

We thanked Mike and his family for their wonderful hospitality, their prayers and for the copy of a book Mike had written, "My Father's Heart", and we retired for the night to rest. I went to sleep thinking about what he had seen and shared. I reflected, too, on the man that I had again had the privilege to spend some time with. I was very impressed with this Father of the Faith and in some ways he reminded me of my last Pastor, Pastor Jim

McKechnie of the Haven Christian Fellowship. Jim, like Mike, was very down to earth with a very practical take on life in general.

WEDNESDAY 20TH JULY

We awoke to another normal Cross Walk morning – rain!

Along the way, the Campbell family – Alan, Louise, Laura and Naomi stopped off with us. They were one of the families that we met when we called at Magherafelt. They were on their way to Newcastle and had come looking for us to encourage us. Such visits and telephone contacts were made immeasurably easier with the use of modern technology and social media.

One of the beauties of Facebook and the Across Ireland page, which Alan was updating on a real time basis, was that people were able to keep in touch or call and see us as they could pin-point easily where we were on the road. This also enabled many to pray regularly for the real-time progress of the team.

A passing driver slowed down and, through an open window, shouted, "Clive Wilson - I need to talk to you!" and without actually coming to a complete stop, hurried on down the road in the direction I had come from - leaving me more than a little puzzled! Less than an hour later the same driver returned, waited for me to finish my half mile stint before asking me to get into the passenger seat of his car. His name was William Kinkead - we had

met some six months previous in Richhill. William was a young Christian who gave his life to God some three years prior. Since that momentous decision that had so radically changed his life, he'd often tried to share his faith with a man he used to do business with at a local shop. None of those conversations seemed to be met with much success because the man showed no real interest or time for anything spiritual - until now!

That very morning, this same man had called William and asked, "Can you come and see me - I need to get my life with God sorted out!" When William suggested he could call after work, the man said that he would much prefer to see him then and there. He needed to do something about it right that moment. William was more than mystified as to what could have brought about such a dramatic turnaround and what would have brought such urgency to his request. So he set off to meet his friend and, on the way, some four miles up the road from the premises, he met me with the cross.

He just knew the cross and the change in thinking were somehow related.

What William discovered was to surprise him

a lot. His friend hadn't even seen the cross but the fact that it had passed within a few metres of the premises where he worked seemed unquestionably to have been the trigger event that was somehow sufficient to induce concern for his soul. William had the privilege of introducing him to his Saviour and lead him in the sinner's prayer.

William said he had been thinking about what had just happened and said to me, upon his return, "Clive, it's almost as if the cross is acting like the bow of a ship and it is leaving an open heaven behind it."

I had heard that before and very recently too! One of the prophecies now to hand, which originated in France on the 15th February 2000, from Dominique Francois, echoed the sentiments of other prophetic texts I had received. Francois recounts, "I have never ever received a vision and a word like the one God seized me with for Ireland. As I was listening to the song 'Oh, consuming fire', I saw the map of Europe circled by a high and thick wall, like a fortified city. Coming from the sea, I saw the [bow] of a big ship – (ice-breaker-type thing) only much bigger, knocking this wall down and making a breakthrough in Europe through Ireland."

This had been the third confirmation specifically detailing the image of the cross acting as a precursor of blessing and leaving in its wake an open heaven over Ireland.

The impact of the cross as it travelled along had, on many occasions on Leg 1 of the Cross Walk, occupied my thoughts. Of particular intrigue was the unusual impact it seemed to have on not only people (stopping and looking or turning vehicles around to come and interrogate us as to our vision) but also, unusually, livestock in the fields.

Their reaction was being noted by the team individually but remained, at that stage, uncommented on. Perhaps this was owing to the fear of being deemed "doting" as we say in Ireland. Consequently, it was a few days before anyone dared to discuss the phenomena. Initially the livestock seemed unusually aware of, and exceptionally startled by the cross's arrival; this might have resulted in them running well away from the roadside hedge. Then however, they followed intently its movement as it passed by, rarely ever taking their attention off the cross. Idle curiosity, one might have thought, but it was so marked at times it just made me wonder if they were in some way sensing something we were unable to.

Were they aware of the sort of changes that William was suggesting he had seen and that had been witnessed in the prayer time the previous evening? The suspicion that there was indeed something very tangible happening in the vicinity of the cross was about to be further enhanced by what would happen next. As William had shared with me the possibility of an open Heaven that was impacting everything in its wake, men and animals included, he said, "Clive, you know, if a bull just realised the sheer power and strength it had, sure no hedge in Ireland would be able to contain it!"

I thought it an unusual comment, albeit we were talking about some of the unusual reactions we had seen in the fields, but we continued our discussion then about what it must have been like as Jesus walked through the countryside and interacted with the local populace. I imagine from what the Gospels record, that Jesus was undoubtedly the most effective communicator to all and sundry. The Gospels record many instances where Jesus took what His listeners would be seeing (e.g. a woman at the offering box in the temple or a farmer sowing seed) and He would use the observed natural event, applying a spiritual lesson to it.

I said to William that I imagined if Jesus were here He would be doing exactly the same as He did when He walked the Middle Eastern countryside some two millennia ago - most definitely. "Jesus Christ, the same yesterday, and today and forever" (Hebrews 13:8, KJV). I added, "That's like us William, as young Christians - if we could only grasp it - Jesus said to His disciples one day as He trained them – "I tell you the truth: It is to your **advantage** that I go away; for if I do not go away, the Helper will not come to you; but if I depart, I will send Him to you" (John 16:7, NKJV).

To the disciples, that must have seemed like the first time they had ever heard Jesus, who said of Himself that He was "the Way, the Truth and the Life," (John 14:6, KJV) saying something they couldn't possibly believe to be true. How could it ever be possible for them to be better off without Him to accompany them on life's journey, what with His feeding the five thousand, healing the sick and raising the dead as he shared and taught them first-hand the principles of the Kingdom of Heaven?

Whilst they could see no reason in the natural how that could ever be true, Jesus explained further the rationale: unless He left to be with His Father in Heaven He would not be able to send the Holy Spirit to come and dwell within their hearts. It was no longer good enough for Jesus to walk along **beside** them, but the arrival of the Holy Spirit to dwell **within** was going to lead to a whole new dimension within their lives.

For many years I have often been struck by the line in Jarrod Cooper's song

King of Kings, Majesty
God of Heaven living in me
Gentle Saviour, Closest friend
Strong Deliverer, beginning and end.
All within me falls at your throne
Your majesty I can but bow
I lay my all before you now,
In royal robes I don't deserve
I live to serve your majesty

(Jarrod Cooper, 1996, Sovereign Lifestyle Music)

The incredible second line with the phenomenal truth 'God of Heaven living IN me' has on many occasions left me contending with a range of emotions ranging from downright disbelieving and flabbergasted to, more often than not, awe-struck in wonder.

As William and I mused on this point I said to him, "Sure William, see what you have just said about the bull? Well, what is true in the natural is similarly true in the spiritual. If you fully realised what actually happened to you three years ago when you repented before God, believed that what Jesus did on Calvary's cross was for you, and received the Holy Spirit and if we Christians could just grasp the enormity of that truth, no denomination or tradition or anything a man could say or do should ever be able stop or restrict God's power now available within us and flowing through us!"

Just then the Team rang me, suggesting that as it was my idea to walk a cross around Ireland, then it might be good if I would come and share the load that day! In fairness we had talked a long time. They suggested coming back to collect me but William wouldn't hear tell of it and offered to run me to where the team had progressed to. As we got out of the car, William (a farmer's son) and I (a farmer's son too) watched the cross moving towards us being carried by a Pastor who spent a long time on his Uncle's farm and what do you know... a bullock, unprovoked by vet needles or polythene sticks, jumps right over a 5-bar gate and stands in the road, right in front of the cross!

My speechless chauffeur could not believe his eyes. He just stood with tears in them asking if I had seen what he just saw? I asked him if he remembered what he had just said in his car only a few minutes earlier. He needed no reminding! As I prayed with him and literally helped him back into his driver's seat, he knew he had seen a truly extraordinary object lesson he would never forget!

Jesus knows how to talk to plasterers, widows, teenagers and farmers' sons at exactly their level. He did years ago and He still connects with people today in ways they can relate to and understand. The Creator of the Universe is a God who is interested in relationship and finds unique ways to meet us on our respective journeys through life and its challenges and hopefully change us in the process, if we let Him.

There are more instances in the Bible of God wanting a relationship with man and wanting to dwell with him, than men wanting a relationship with Him. From the Garden of Eden, where in the cool of the day He came

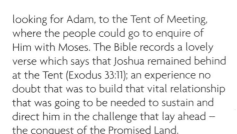

looking for Adam, to the Tent of Meeting, where the people could go to enquire of Him with Moses. The Bible records a lovely verse which says that Joshua remained behind at the Tent (Exodus 33:11); an experience no doubt that was to build that vital relationship that was going to be needed to sustain and direct him in the challenge that lay ahead – the conquest of the Promised Land.

In the New Testament, John records that "the Word became flesh and dwelt among us" (John 1:14, ESV). God is on the lookout for precious souls; He earnestly seeks a living and real relationship with all who will take time out from their busy lives chasing materialism and position to walk with Him a while.

I love the account of Enoch, who the Bible simply records "walked faithfully with God: then he was no more, because God took him away" (Genesis 5: 24, NIV). Was it so rare for God in Heaven to find a single soul who would simply take time to walk with Him? It certainly was a relationship that Scripture records as wholly unusual.

As this young convert drove away, I prayed he would be used to liberate many in his area and show, through the power of the Holy Spirit, the need to step outside the confinement of people and restriction of past religious experiences.

Lord...
Set your church free to clear hurdles.
Set your church free to break boundaries.
Set your church free to get on the road.
Set your church free to meet others and encourage all they meet along life's journey.

Towards the end of that evening we arrived in Dromore, where we met the Youth For Christ (YFC) team who were doing street evangelism work as part a week's outreach with a team from America. We held a short time of sharing the vision in their wonderfully well-equipped outreach bus and together we walked the cross into the centre of town and prayed at the centre.

We talked and prayed into various concerns in their locality as they shared them, including a sense that suicidal thinking was operational in the thinking and minds of some of the young people. One young leader from the area, felt that to be particularly true. As we left the centre of town and were walking back towards the park where the young people regularly met, I offered to go and pray with her at her church. Whilst she had no key, I felt strongly impressed to walk around the church (the Church of Ireland Cathedral for Down and Connor). I only made it to the first corner as I was beginning to walk clockwise around the church when she stopped me and said, "This is strange!" During an open Sunday night service three weeks ago she felt compelled to walk around the church. When she got to this very spot she felt her attention directed to look at the river and saw a scene of death in the river – she did not describe exactly the detail of what she had seen but she heard simply the words, "The river's cursed". She hadn't known what to do with that thought.

I shared with her about some very real experiences that others had encountered in Ireland, when cleaning up river areas both physically and spiritually. On our journey with the Cross, the team had often

prayed at significant landmark points like rivers, which at times not only provide physical boundaries between areas but are also of clear spiritual significance. We were to see this very clearly on the final leg of the walk.

Once again, as we had done at various other stops on the journey, the team prayed for the specific location that she had identified and the waterway concerned. On our way back to the park we also prayed at another location where a local clairvoyant had moved in and was attempting to establish their business. We heard later that before the end of the week that specific property was put up for sale!

Spiritual opposition comes at many levels – this young leader had recently been diagnosed with an eye disorder, which she noticed was all the more pronounced after she had committed herself to study her Bible more. We prayed for her and the entire YFC team that night and left after thoroughly enjoying a barbecue with the young people in the park.

YFC have had a desire to see their mission extended and operational in all 32 counties of Ireland. Project 32 connects young people from all over the world – training and serving in outreach programs right across the island of Ireland. YFC were inviting young people to join them in Belfast in 2012 to "take their place in what God is doing in this incredible island." I liked their invitation and their inclusiveness.

We returned late to Closkelt where once again we stayed with Mike Oman who had asked us if we would offer a hand to lay a concrete floor early the next morning before we set off on our journey. We were more than happy to oblige, particularly as this week we had on board a team member who had spent 10 years laying concrete floors. God at work in the small detail again very evident on this leg of the crosswalk!

THURSDAY 21ST JULY

Our initial enthusiasm for the flooring project was somewhat dampened by the early start but that paled into insignificance when we saw the concrete lorry disgorging so much concrete in front of the property I felt there was enough to floor a silo never mind a front living room! Dismay was further added to by the fact that every last cubic metre of it needed to be shovelled! Mike, at 64 years young and with the energy levels of a man half his age, had already been hard at work on site from 6am and seemed unphased!

We began our task believing we were going to see the miracle of the feeding of the 5000 in reverse and assumed Mike knew of a very deep rabbit hole in the centre of his room that would require this massive mountain of concrete.

Brian (of building expertise fame and alluded to earlier) confirmed our suspicions that the proverbial rabbit hole did not exist and should we continue to cart in the concrete to the front room there might only be enough head clearance for a height-challenged rabbit between our new rapidly rising floor level and the already low ceiling!

When we stopped for refreshments mid-morning, Mike, still mystified by the miscalculation, said to his credit, "Whilst often we may make mistakes – God never does!" Together as a group around the kitchen table, we prayed seeking a solution. I just felt the simple thought, 'You have your dad's pickup.'

After tea break, when we again began shovelling, I mentioned the thought to Mike that perhaps we could move the excess concrete for someone to use on their own site? He said, "No I don't think so, I have a name in mind but do not have their mobile telephone number. They live a couple of miles away – I wonder if you could give me a lift over to their place and see if they could use some of the additional concrete?" This we did, to discover to our delight that they could in fact use some concrete for a building that was currently under construction and would call and collect it in the next ten minutes with a large forwarder. The unexpected blessing was that they knew something about YWAM's work already and they were happy to pay their share of the load of concrete!

So many times we watched the Lord at work in the small detail of one another's lives. "Truly I tell you, if anyone says to this mountain, 'Go, throw yourself into the sea,' and does not doubt in his heart but believes that what they say will happen, it will be done for them" (Mark 11:23 NIV)

As a team, we may not have the decreased the size of the Irish Sea, so to speak, but together we did share another amazing provision from the goodness of God in the lives of ordinary men and women (well, four tired men at least – the women would probably have measured it right first time around and missed out on all the all the muscle building and faith-building adventure!)

With the floor finally finished and starting to set, the team got back on the road to walk on to Banbridge via Corbet. Mid-afternoon we met and prayed with Stephen, the new Elim Pastor, in the centre of Banbridge. Stephen quipped that there had to be something special at work to get him down and bent on his, then, very stiff knees! After that we enjoyed a very welcome cup of coffee to warm our bones.

As happened on many occasions, people from Richhill Elim came to share the load, to fellowship and encourage us on our journey. That night we ended our walk in Gilford. Originally we had planned to park up the caravan in the car park in the centre of town but Alan, on the way into town, met a lady, Linda, out walking her Yorkshire terrier dog.

Again, as with so many encounters on the Cross Walk, Linda indicated that it was always her oldest daughter that would walk the dog but today just happened to be the one and only time she was there to take the dog out to the end of the driveway. As a result of that encounter, Alan was extended an invitation to park our caravan at the back of their house. However, before we were to accept that invitation we spent time talking to the young people in Gilford in the car park. The first thing I noted that all appeared to be dressed in grey hoodies! When I asked if this was the official gang attire for the 'in crowd' they started laughing, as up until that point they hadn't realised how similar they all looked. We talked with many – some wanted the opportunity to feel the weight of the cross, some mocking, some embarrassed, some intrigued, some drugged, some drunk. One young man whose nickname I seem to remember was 'Horsepower' (don't ask me!) discussed with us the difference between the power of one horse and one cross. One Horsepower lost!

After some wonderful hospitality with Trevor and Linda and their little daughter, we settled down for the night.

FRIDAY 22ND JULY

The team set off the next morning for Tandragee whilst I headed back to do a radio interview with my friend Nathan on Shine 102.4FM. It was when I was with Nathan in Uganda that all this had begun. He ended up affording us almost an hour of airtime, filling his listeners in on the vision and the progress to-date. It was the last time we were ever to be in a studio together.

I recalled the first Shine FM interview he ever did with me about the Ark of the Covenant, in which surprise questions were launched my way with the innocent smile a cherub would have been pleased with and he sat there as I battled my way to recover composure and furnish him with the most lucid answer I could as quickly as I could in response to his searching questions. He certainly kept you on your toes! He later batted away my protestations, saying that whilst interviews for community radio need not be as rigorous as Jeremy Paxman of Newsnight fame might conduct, they still needed to be real nonetheless! I said nothing.

After the interview, I drove to catch up with the rapidly advancing cross, which had been caught that morning on a speed camera!

The previous night we had talked about going through Portadown but when in Tandragee, the team felt strongly to take the cross-country route. I found myself on the back roads near the village Hamiltonsbawn and by now driving on fumes! The previous day the Lord had prompted us to empty our pockets and give what we had to meet a specific need and so, with absolutely no money and the one and only filling station between us and the finish point just 200 metres away, I was praying "Lord, we need fuel and FAST!!!"

I caught up with the team on the outskirts of the village and we stopped for a bite of lunch. I hadn't even had time to explain to the team our latest predicament when a lady driver pulls up to a halt and abandon parks (nothing new there then!) to enquire how we were progressing. Margaret, a lady from our local congregation, reached me £20 for "refreshment." I told her what I had been praying and that the van was well, well below empty and it needed refreshment more than me! She was very much 'in the spirit'. She was both amazed and moved. She then reached for her chequebook and told me to fill the tank. I thanked her but told her that now she was reacting emotionally to the need. What she had done initially was all God had wanted her to do and by being obedient she had already blessed us enormously.

We pulled into the filling station nearby and by the time I had walked a further 1000m another precious parishioner contributed what filled the tank to the top! Edith White was a grandmother and, despite a heart condition, she had waited to carry the cross up the main street of Hamiltonsbawn with me. She later shared at our church service the following Sunday morning that when she had finished her stint through the village she had sensed a very clear healing and strengthening flow through her.

Later that afternoon I even had my oldest parishioner, 82 year old Seamus McCarthy, carry the cross with me for part of the way ON A ZIMMER FRAME! Wow! I was thankful for his efforts and with all who came to encourage and share the load.

Friends from church met us regularly, often with much needed supplies. Whilst it is good to be encouraged and good to be prayed for and good for someone to walk a while with you and better still when they bear the weight of the cross, it is very hard to beat a freshly baked chocolate cake! **Thank you to everyone who showed their love in so, so many ways.**

Our arrival route this time allowed us to overlook the City. I pondered again what Patrick must have felt when he too reached Armagh and began to appraise its religious influence and power as well as its potential to launch a whole new Bible based faith for all the people of the island and beyond.

Another of the prophecies that I had studied near Strangford introduced me to a brand new phrase - 'Peregrinatio pro Dei amore' (Wandering for the love of God) an Irish tradition from the sixth century onwards. Often people in those times were so

phenomenally impacted by the message of the love of God that nothing else mattered nor was of concern to them, save sharing the message of the Gospel of Jesus Christ with the wider world. Many left Ireland and travelled to far-off lands to be a witness by the way they lived.

Some of the prophecies perused at the outset of this Leg, including Cramer's, see that day returning, where the young people in Ireland will be used mightily to follow the same path and share the most important thing the world needs to see genuinely in action - God's love.

St Patrick's faith, all those years back, caused many to wonder. His depiction of God as a God of relationship and one who walks beside us has urged many thereafter not just to wonder but to wander as well. I was just another one.

Our arrival at Navan Fort from the East at 6.50pm completed Across Walk Leg 3, this time in sunshine and we finished it with our usual prayer. Outside St Patrick's Cathedral, we enjoyed fellowship again with all the welcome team and Beth Heron with some intercessors from Tres Dias (a ministry that works to help strengthen Christians in their walk with Christ) who had travelled from Belfast to stand with us and encourage us on to complete the final leg.

The next leg would be the longest and the toughest test yet, but for now we were able to return home with the fallacy that we were now three quarters the way through; one more big push would see the project complete. "Downhill all the way from here" someone said, but looking at a map of Ireland, and the big push up from Waterford, it didn't look that down hill - not at all!

CROSS WALK LEG 3:
Strangford to Navan Fort, Armagh | 57 miles

Saggart

Blessington

Baltinglass

Tullow

Bunclody

Ballycarney

Enniscorthy

Oylegate

Wexford

The Longest Leg

CROSS WALK LEG 4
Wexford to Armagh

The early preparations for the final push up through Ireland were fraught with frustration.

The YFC team in Dromore had offered us their purpose-built bus for the final leg and so we travelled over to collect it late on the Saturday evening but all attempts to kick-start it into life met with no success whatsoever. Despite all our efforts to persuade it to join us on the journey, it had clearly decided it was going nowhere! In the midst of that frustration and a tangle of jump leads, my Sunday morning guest speaker phoned to cancel at the what was now the eleventh hour literally, leaving a whole new sermon to be uncovered overnight – It must be Cross Walk week again!

After the congregation had endured and I had survived (just) a hastily constructed sermon, we relaxed a fraction more through the evening service, which had had a bit more prior planning. The Sunday night service was one where I had the opportunity to dedicate to God our most recent arrival into church - a little baby boy called Noah. One of the extraordinary privileges that you have as a Pastor is being invited into people's lives to share with them in their happiest occasions (as in this instance) or when, for example, they as a family are grieving the loss of a precious loved family member. They are unique moments and being asked to serve in a pastoral role is an extraordinarily privileged position.

Following that service and supper, the team set the compass point due south and headed off for the final outward bound journey to the coast, arriving at Kilmore Quays, Wexford in the South East of Ireland at 3:30am. Looking at the map, this leg was clearly the longest and, from what I could see, it appeared ALL uphill!

MONDAY 8TH AUGUST

The day started out dry and, with the glorious sunshine lifting our spirits, we began the long trek north. We had only managed thirty metres before being engaged by a local cycling club who were taking the benefit of the holiday weekend to stretch their legs and cover some road miles.

I walked a full 360° around the first roundabout, unaware of their watchful eye from where they had pulled in for a

breather. Intrigued, and assuming I must be a foreigner and lost, they asked why I had just circumnavigated the roundabout and did I need help? I joked that it was always a good thing to walk around roundabouts when you are claiming mileage! It was however an unusual moment that, whilst starting as a joke, was later that morning to take on a new significance.

I was enthralled with some of the amazing thatched cottages in Kilmore Quays and

as a team we continued walking north, with our sleepy heads seriously locked on our mid-morning caffeine infusion. En route, we saw a large number of roadside commemorative crosses at several locations where, presumably, accidents had occurred and loved ones had been lost, none more so than in this part of Ireland.

I was doing the final cross-carrying stint before coffee and was only a few hundred yards away from meeting the team again when my attention was captured by a cross in the grounds of a local chapel.

This cross was different because it told very simply but very effectively a lot more of the story of the crucifixion of that Good Friday some 2000 years ago in Jerusalem - the ladder, the nails, the sponge, the spear all in their own way added to the object lesson.

As I stopped to take a photograph, a man from a small road-side restaurant nearby asked me did I want a cup of coffee. I thanked him but said "No", knowing the team had 'a brew' already underway just up the road. As I turned to continue my journey, a little boy ran across the road and held on to the bottom of the cross. It turned out he was the grandson of the man who had just invited me to stay for a cuppa and this little lad was clearly intent on not letting go of his grip of my more portable cross.

He just wouldn't let go; it was almost as if he too wanted me to stay, though he didn't say anything. I asked him his name and was met with his first word... "Noah". I thought to myself, that name rings a bell! There was something about the encounter and the fact that just 12 hours previous I had dedicated a baby called Noah that encouraged me to say 'No....aaaaahhh maybe I will!' to his Granda's offer of a coffee after all. Maybe if I was quick the team wouldn't notice and I reasoned that a double caffeine shot was probably the minimum requirement that morning anyway!

We crossed the road and sat down inside their restaurant and I engaged in conversation with Noah's grandfather. There we spent several hours talking about the family history. He was a priest who, many years before, had been forced to relinquish his call to the priesthood as a consequence of the arrival of a love child. His subsequent marriage and the arrival of a little girl was to lead to two decades of intense personal recrimination. A life lived full of regrets that were not the child's fault, but ultimately led to enormous pain for all the precious lives involved. In life, as with so many families all round the world, the "if only" of the past can continually haunt the present. Apparently they have a saying in Germany, *"Wenn das Wörtchen 'wenn' nicht wär"* - "If only noone had ever come up with that little word 'if'" How true! **But all that said, the God of Scripture is portrayed so often as a God of the second chance. One of the most famous stories ever told by Jesus about the prodigal son resonates down through the centuries and it still breathes hope and brings solace to many**

who wish they had not squandered what had been entrusted to them.

As we talked, many tears flowed and eventually together we got down on our knees on the floor of the restaurant and I asked him to pray Isaiah 45:8. Immediately upon so doing, his second daughter shared in floods of tears about her life, her love of fashion, the impact that a recent trip to Zimbabwe had had upon her thinking and of her desire to be right with God. That day, within minutes of Isaiah 45:8 being released over their property, in a heartfelt moment of surrender, she offered her life completely to the will of God. **It was an incredibly powerful moment and perhaps one of the most emotional experiences on the entire Cross Walk journey. God was already starting to heal wounds that were years old and restore to spiritual headship a much wounded heart.**

As we talked, the former priest shared the fact that some 3-4 weeks before each Good Friday he had always nursed the notion to make a cross and walk with it to commemorate the significance of that all-important day, but given his past, he never felt he ever could. Neither did he... until that day!

I asked him to share with me the opportunity and privilege of walking with the cross along the road through his county. This he did with a very glad heart and blessed the team enormously as he did so. His being able to do that represents, I believe, a landmark moment in the life of an ordinary human being discovering that God is more interested in our relationship with Him than ever in anything we can do for Him. It is not about the mechanics of ministry or position or prestige or pride. It is just walking in obedience with a loving Heavenly Father who never overlooks sin but understands frailty and extends forgiveness more readily than often we are prepared to seek it, let alone grant it to ourselves.

Paul in his letter to the Romans wants his readers to connect with that truth when he points out in Romans 8: 1-2 "Therefore, there is now no condemnation for those who are in Christ Jesus, because through Christ Jesus the law of the Spirit who gives life has set you free from the law of sin and death" (NIV). I once heard someone describe to me the fact that in Christianity you are either 'up' or 'getting up.' **The enemy of our souls always wants us to remain downtrodden and un-restored but our God restores and rescues lives always.**

The Apostle John reveals an important truth of two ways believers can defeat the ploys of the enemy whilst in this world: "And they overcame him by the blood of the Lamb and by the word of their testimony" (Revelation 12:1, KJV). The testimony of an overcomer will bring much glory to God and so the enemy is intent on robbing from a man his testimony, as he knows that will cause him to be an ineffective witness within his family, his church and his community. **The tussle to taint your testimony is relentless and lifelong.**

During our time together, we talked about the spiritual history of the area. In bygone times, this part of Ireland was often dark and troubled. At Carnsore Point, a headland in the very South East corner of County Wexford, child sacrifice was evidenced. In contemporary history, extraordinary divisiveness was one of the alleged hallmarks of the peoples who resided in this area of Ireland. Underperformance on the sport fields and in the economy were all features that cropped up in wide-ranging discussion as we talked with locals along way. Someone even alluded to the fact that, not so terribly long ago, a local artist had turned a carved tree trunk upside down, with roots skyward, in the centre of the roundabout at Kilmore Quays depicting a very unnatural, very upside down world. In some senses, his artistic statement seemed to underscore that here, as indeed in much of the rest of Ireland, we have got distorted perspectives and priorities upside down.

It reminded me somewhat of the world in the days of the early Church in the Book of Acts. In those days the natural order had become so distorted yet appeared the norm to many, so much so that when the disciples arrived with the good news of the gospel of Jesus Christ, the local community were complaining vociferously. Acts 17:6 states "And when they could not find them, they dragged Jason and some of the brothers before the city authorities, shouting, 'These men who have turned the world upside down have come here also'" (ESV).

Back to contemporary Irish times, the upside down tree sculpture had apparently engendered more local outrage than praise. It is encouraging to hear that, despite a past that had somehow lost out on the ideals of love, unity and community, people in this part of the world still recognise natural order needs once again to be restored. Maybe I look at life too simplistically, but I tend to see my God as turning the land the right way up!

Maybe that day He was - the roundabout that had once displayed the unnatural, upside down dead tree sculpture that had upset the locals, was the very roundabout I had circumnavigated with the cross at the outset! Interestingly the only one meted out for special treatment on all our travels!

STRAWBERRIES FOR SALE

In this corner of Ireland the soft fruit industry clearly plays an important role in the local agri-business sector and this was the showcase time of the season. Round every corner, roadside pitches were plying their trade and selling their best local agricultural produce including strawberries, raspberries and all manner of fresh fruit and new season potatoes. We passed many on our travels that day, little wonder Wexford is referred to as Strawberry County. At one particular pitch I came across a girl who was reading a book. The day had been slow and she had progressed further through her novel than perhaps her boss would have wished! Strawberries sat unsold. I felt I should set down the cross and chat to her. As we talked

it was clear she had many questions on her mind. A traveller stopped to ask for directions and she suggested I move the cross in case someone tripped on it and so together we leaned it up against the side of her strawberry pitch as she continued to ask questions.

She began to share something of her personal journey through life, her quest for fun on the party scene, her subsequent battle with illness, for which apparently there was no ultimate cure, and the treatment for the symptoms had ramifications for her as a young woman some of which would have the potential to be life changing. In some ways, I was reminded of Cross Leg 2 and the young couple in Kilrea.

As we talked she kept crying and as she tried to share with me passers-by kept would interrupt us at pertinent points in the conversation. In frustration, I prayed, "Lord, sort this!" I think of Nehemiah's flash prayer to heaven when the King asked what was troubling him. When an earthly King, then so revered and so powerful, asks you a question, palace etiquette would have demanded a rapid reply.

Nehemiah 2:3-5 states, "Then the king said to me, "What do you request?" *So I prayed to the God of heaven and I said to the king, "If it pleases the king, and if your servant has found favour in your sight, I ask that you send me to Judah, to the city of my fathers' tombs, that I may rebuild it"* (NKJV).

Your Heavenly Father knows the situation you find yourself even before you yourself know you are going to walk into it!

Well, what ensued after my prayer was comical! It seemed like everybody in the county decided they would make jam that evening! The strawberries began to sell like hot cakes – now callers were taking significant quantities home with them. I waited in her wee weather shelter and passed the time reading the credits and introduction to the novel she had been spent her day engrossed in - a crime thriller by the author Ian Rankin entitled ... *'Knots & Crosses'*.

After about twenty minutes, all supplies for her shift were sold with the exception of four punnets on the table. Two ladies arrived simultaneously. The girl, somewhat dizzy from the recent flurry of sales activity, turned to me and said "Clive, one of these two ladies is going to be disappointed!" (an assumption based upon the average off-take quantity of all her recent callers). The penultimate caller asked "Can I have one punnet, please?" and the final lady...?

"I have driven past 5 or 6 strawberry sellers around that roundabout up there and back to here because apparently these are the best! I need 3!"

With the stock all sold and still half an hour before her shift was due to finish it gave me the perfect opportunity to talk uninterrupted with her without annoying her boss. I ran up the road and collapsed the sign saying, 'Strawberries for Sale' face down. Walking back towards her she came running towards me and asked me the most unusual thing anyone ever has... "Are you God?"

For a moment I was completely astonished at her enquiry and asked why on earth she would even think that. She replied, "Ever since you arrived with the cross, the hair has been standing on the back of my neck!" Again and again she posed the same question. When I assured her that I most certainly was not, she asked "Why do I feel this way? What has just happened?" We sat and talked, until the end of her shift, about how God desires to be in relationship with us and how, through his Holy Spirit, He makes his dwelling place within our hearts. We spoke about verses in the New Testament, like 1 Corinthians 6:19 "Do you not know that your body is the temple of the Holy Spirit who is in you, whom you have from God, and you are not your own?" (NKJV).

I shared my experience of God's love with her and how it related to the particulars of her life and prayed for the healing she needed. As I left she promised to buy a Bible the very next morning and read it to start to discover more about this man Jesus and what He had done for her. I smiled as I left the tearful young woman thinking to myself, "Lord you do all things well!"

As I walked away from that encounter, I marvelled at the degree to which the cross had unravelled a life that was incredibly knotted up.

God designed strawberries and can certainly make them sell!

God designed this lady's life and can certainly make her well!

We prayed as a team in the centre of Wexford and later that evening as I was settling down we reflected on the events of the day. I recalled the fact that the strawberry seller had helped me lift and set the cross up against the side of her weather shelter and The chorus of the now famous song "The Power Of The Cross" by Stuart Townend and Keith Getty echoed around in my head,

"This, the power of the cross:
Christ became sin for us.
Took the blame, bore the wrath—
We stand forgiven at the cross."
(Stuart Townend & Keith Getty, 2005, Thankyou Music)

A power unchanged, no matter how far in time we move away the momentous events in Jerusalem. In particular too, I thought much about what Noah's grandfather had said that whilst Wexford may have had a troubled past it had also often been described more positively as the "Gateway to Europe". I prayed that once again young Saints and scholars from this part of Ireland would leave these shores wandering with the love of God burning brightly in their hearts.

TUESDAY 9TH AUGUST

The next morning we had a kick-start breakfast of bacon butties and 4 Jaffa Cakes! Probably not the ideal breakfast nutritionally but it got us up and on the road and heading towards Oylegate, where I spent some time sharing with two ladies from the Irish Countrywomen's Association, but all to no avail! It turned out they were both stiff-necked people with hearts of stone!

Later that afternoon, the team arrived into Enniscorthy. Crossing the Slaney river Alan stopped to pray, as he was accustomed, and immediately sensed that this had been a river area that had seen much death. Following his prayer at the bridge he took the cross up the very steep hill towards the town centre and prayed on the high ground in the centre of town.

On his way back down his attention was drawn to a set of premises that signalled to all and sundry that they were interested in

helping all those "Touched by Suicide" – that's what the sign on the premises said.

Alan spoke with two ladies in the shop – Kay, a local, who had sadly lost two sons, to suicide and Denise, her friend, who together co-founded their charity to raise funds for counselling services for people who are affected by the suicide of a loved one or are suicidal themselves. The second-hand shop was the mainstay cash cow of the charity and the shop sign "Touched by Suicide" didn't airbrush the cause. Some people had been uncomfortable about the directness of the shop sign and there were even attempts to have it changed. What drives Kay is the wish to prevent others suffering the pain that she experienced following the deaths of her two beloved sons.

Alan asked them if the river held any specific significance and was informed that the year previous, eight suicides had occurred in the

river through drowning in the space of just one week. Enniscorthy and nearby Tullen were perceived by them as "pockets of suicide". Kay runs a 24 hour hotline on her own phone offering access to counsellors. She often gets calls from people saying, "I'm standing on the bridge in Enniscorthy and I'm going to jump". Kay doesn't live too far from the bridge and she goes there when she's needed. Indeed, she had been to the edge of the river herself.

Having walked away from a point at the river that depicted death and sadness, our walk north along the same river was, in contrast, bathed in glorious sunshine and we enjoyed lunch in the beautiful setting which refreshed our souls.

BARRY'S BISCUITS

By teatime that evening, we still had a few more miles to go to meet our daily target. When I was rounding a roundabout a young man called Barry caught sight of the cross. Understanding just how hot the afternoon was, he felt compelled to go to a local shop and purchase some provisions. When eventually he returned I was no longer carrying the cross but had transferred it to Chris. When Barry arrived with the selected supplies Chris jested that since he had no hands to carry his gift, Barry should drive a little farther up the road to give it to us at the caravan. Somewhat taken aback by the fact that there were more than one of us in the team and feeling he had not bought sufficient supplies for that eventuality, he took some persuasion to make his way to us, particularly as he was already late for football training. Nonetheless he did and so...

I met a very badly dressed Barry, bearing a bottle of water, chicken sandwiches and manna from heaven indeed, in the form of... wait for it... a packet of Jaffa Cakes! **There are significant moments in life that one remembers. This will always be one of them for me. Someone arriving to offer support, having never met you before but turning up with your all-time favourite biscuit on the planet AND exactly when energy levels are flagging! Often God shows us in small, very practical ways that you're on the right road, at the right time, doing exactly the right thing. In a gentle way, it just felt like one of those small moments packed with significance.**

Barry again intimated to me, as I thanked him,

that he was already late for football training and needed to move quickly but nonetheless something intrigued him about what we were doing. I could sense a tugging at his heart to stay and ask questions. He was a deep thinker and well-read and one question led to another and another and another!

As so often we saw on our journey, when the Spirit of God arrests a man in his tracks, it is almost as if one of his feet has been tacked to the tarmac! Whilst his mind knows he has to be somewhere and his head tells him he is late, there are specific times when the call upon a life is so strong it they are almost compelled to stay and listen. We had talked for quite some time when eventually I offered him a seat in the caravan, an offer he accepted despite at the same time indicating he was still in a rush and now even later for football training! Probably a whole hour after he had shared the Jaffa Cakes with us and after we had shared truth from God's word with him, he was still intently listening to God's truth. He had studied other faiths.

He went to mass; his mum didn't as she just prayed to God herself and said that "you

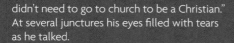

didn't need to go to church to be a Christian." At several junctures his eyes filled with tears as he talked.

When Barry heard we were doing a live radio interview later in the week on Spirit FM in Dublin, he was again intrigued. He said that he had been flicking through the radio stations the previous Wednesday and, for the first time ever, he had listened to it. Again, God ahead of time was preparing a heart to receive the good news of the gospel of Jesus Christ.

Like the plasterer we met on Leg 3, Barry indicated that he never usually travelled on this road. He said, "Clive, I have never heard it put more simply. I want to ask Jesus into my life. Is there a prayer card I need to read out?" He seemed to be expecting to see a short written prayer that had been penned by someone else and that one could keep in a pocket to pray repeatedly, 'just to be sure'.

Just that morning, Alan and I had been discussing prayer and specifically quotations from C. H. Spurgeon and Tertullian. The former said in lectures to his students, "be sure that free prayer is that most scriptural and should be the most excellent form of public supplication" and the latter stated that "we pray without a prompter because it's from the heart". With that chat very fresh in my mind, I suggested to Barry that, rather than use a formal prayer written by someone else, he could pray his own words pointing out that faltering words wouldn't get in the way of a really sincere heart.

And so he prayed what was on his heart.

It was simple.

It was thoughtful.

It was sincere.

It was touching.

It was emotional.

It was another miracle of new birth.

And then...

just before he finished praying...

He simply included a request that was so unique, so incredible it left me dumbfounded!

He unbelievably asked God to give Manchester United a really good season and help them to do well.

Amen.

He then closed his eyes and leaned his head against the wall of the caravan behind him and no one spoke for some time. He then opened his eyes and said "Clive I have an incredible sense of peace."

I said "Peace? Peace? I am raging! I am a Chelsea supporter and (with a sweep of my left hand towards Chris on the caravan step on my left) this clown, who has been praying for you Barry, for the last 40 minutes, is a Liverpool supporter!"

97

I told him he had committed what I would consider almost the 'unpardonable sin' hereafter referred to as a 'Barry Blunder' and I said that I would be asking God to strike that last request from the record!

We laughed and he presumed I was joking! With powerful young pray-ers like Barry on the opposing side, the Chelsea contingent would need to pull their socks up and fast. We might have to settle for second place in the Premiership!

As he left to catch what was probably now just the tail end of his training session, I reflected on what was easily by far and away the most non-religious moment I had ever experienced in my life! There were no clerical collars; there were no robes; there was no incense; there were no books of Common prayer - just an ordinary guy, with a genuine heart putting his hand for the first time ever, into the hand of the God who created and designed him from before the foundation of the world. It was a miraculous moment to witness. It always is.

On we walked and that day we finished in Ballycarney on the east bank of the River Slaney. We parked the caravan up on waste ground beside the local Church of Ireland church and headed off to the nearby truck stop where we had the first meal out for the team of the Across Ireland Cross Walk so far, in the roadside cafe. It was bliss - salmon, two steaks and three showers!

The meal that day had been provided for us by a priest we had encountered along the way. Over dinner that night we talked again through our encounter with him.

He had relayed to us how, on the previous morning, his normal early morning routine had been altered by events to the extent that, several hours later than usual, he went to get a paper in his local shop. While waiting to be served, he was amazed when he felt what he described as "an anointing" pass the shop. He paid for his paper and stepped quickly outside to see the cross disappearing out of view. He turned his car around to catch up with the team wanting to discover a little bit more about what we were doing. In his

initial conversation with Chris and Alan, he indicated that he was on the way to see the Bishop but promised to return to speak with us later that night.

Due to unforeseen circumstances, he did not reconnect with us until after lunch the following day. We sat down over a cup of tea in the caravan and he shared with us something of his journey of faith. He has involvement with and responsibility for many lives in his parish of Crossabeg, Wexford. We talked of many things including a mutual acquaintance that we both knew, Shirley Bowers of Arise Ministries.

Shirley, from Huntingdon in England, after studying some of the history of her predecessor Oliver Cromwell and some of the horrific damage that he unleashed on the people of Ireland, felt strongly compelled to visit Ireland and the locations that Cromwell had encamped, but with an "opposite spirit". Rather than barging into cities and towns by force, she came by invitation and prayed for forgiveness and reconciliation. This priest had been responsible for setting up a ministry visit to Barbados for her to see the "red legs", apparently so called due to the effects of the tropical sun on their fair-skinned legs. They were an oppressed minority that for many years had been subjected to intolerable lifestyles. Whilst not exclusively so, some descended from Irish ancestry, after being forcibly shipped there under Cromwell's rule as 'white slaves'.

We spent some time that afternoon talking about Isaiah 45:8 and the release of righteousness. We shared about God's call in our lives, the responsibility that had been entrusted to us and we prayed for God's work in this part of Ireland. As we prayed, I could just feel the pain in his heart for the people. **I was sorry to say goodbye to him. I felt he had a very gentle, humble spirit and heart. As he left, he thanked us for being a real blessing within his parish and pressed a gift into our hands to buy a meal at the end of the day. It was the first sit down meal we had been provided with and meant that the beef ravioli could stay in the tin for another night!**

With the debrief over for the day and thanks said to God we were just settling down for the night when three local farmers descended upon us and asked "Is there a camping sign at the entrance?" (gesturing to the piece of waste ground upon which we were then parked.) I indicated there wasn't and they, presumably assuming we were members of the travelling fraternity told us the guards would be round in 10 minutes if we did not rapidly remove ourselves lock, stock and barrel! We beat a hasty retreat to a nearby lorry park. Sleep was always difficult to secure on the road but in the corner of a lorry park, when you have the first lorry pulling its trailer out of the park at 2:40am (Murphy's Law as always ensured that that was the one right beside where we had hurriedly parked the caravan), that was the end of sleep for that night!

WEDNESDAY 10TH AUGUST

Just after the cross set off northward bound, I was interviewed by Paul on South East Radio and, for twenty minutes, had a wonderful opportunity to share the journey that we were on. During the programme, we had a lot of listener feedback all of which was positive. We even had one caller who phoned in to say that she had seen us with the cross praying in the centre of Oylegate. She later that same day learned from a government press announcement that they now would no longer be undertaking to build the proposed bypass around Oylegate and so it was being shelved for now. We knew nothing of the local politics on the ground but the listener certainly saw it as some sort of divine intervention, thus no doubt allowing their little community to remain a busy thoroughfare for passing trade!

Subsequent to that radio interview, many people came to see us along the road and we prayed for them, we prayed for skin conditions like eczema, we shared our testimony with many and gladly received some offers of assistance. One mum, who was very engaged and interested, said she would meet us farther on the road later with a supply of homemade treats just for the occasion, which she did. Welcome indeed!

Whilst climbing a significant incline, I stopped and chatted to a man who said he was from Derry and who was leaning over a farm gate and admiring the rolling countryside, the harvest scene and the River Slaney that sprawled far in the distance beneath us.

It was that gentleman that first filled me in about the rioting that had broken out in London. Whilst on the walk we had been immersed in the local detail and issues which were to hand and so to some degree we had been isolated from the outside world. It came as a significant shock when he simply said, "They're pulling London apart and it's spreading fast!" We felt a million miles removed in the quiet peace of the Irish countryside.

We kept pushing north and eventually arrived on the outskirts of Bunclody. Alan was doing the lift of the cross through town. Chris and I meantime had been standing admiring just how tidy the graveyard on the outskirts of town was. No doubt it had been prepared by many families from the area for Cemetery Sunday.

Whilst there, the local Gardaí asked what we were about and, as a result of that discussion, they invited us to call into the Gardaí station on the route out of town. This we did and we had a wonderful lunch with local Gardaí officers. **This was our first face-to-face encounter with the law. More were to come!**

Meanwhile Alan was a long time coming. He had stopped to pray in the town centre where he was immediately surrounded by four or five people and then quickly twelve. The locals asked what he was doing; some asked for a prayer for healing; some came to raise a riot, shouting and creating a real stir.

To further add to the confusion, Trevor Stevenson from the Fields of Life Charity also arrived in the middle of the melee asking

to speak to me! Trevor did so much work in Uganda, Africa, building schools and digging fresh water wells. Even if Alan had known where we were, he would have been too busy to direct him!

Alan politely asked the main antagonist of the mob to wait while he spoke to two locals, one of whom was called Tom. The man declined the offer to wait and continued to raise his voice. Alan prayed. Tom meanwhile turned to his fellow local and simply stated, "God is in control, beware as Christ will return like a thief in the night!" That statement silenced the clamour. Then Alan, as he so often did, managed to control the group and share his faith with as many as would listen. What bemused him somewhat was the fact that the locals who attacked the cross were engaged by locals who believed in it and he was left an astonished onlooker at times in the discussions that followed – somewhat reminiscent of the apostle Paul who, everywhere he went, created a riot or a revival! May Bunclody have its revival Lord!

One man stood at a distance and, unknown to Alan, observed everything that was going on - Alan's answers offered to the questions posed and also his conduct during a pressurised encounter.

He said nothing but walked away.

We now had more miles behind than in front of us!

THURSDAY 11TH AUGUST

We arrived in Tullow and the team prayed in the town and for the people and the area. Upon leaving town, a man in a 4x4 wound the window down and shouted out to Alan, "I need to speak to you, I'll be at the end of the road where it's safe." A Garda car had stopped us on the road from Tullow to Baltinglass and told us to be careful because the road was very dangerous. It took some way for the caller to find a safe place to pull in and indeed that was the very place where Chris and I were waiting for Alan to arrive.

His name was Mick. He was single and farmed an organic sheep farm. To survive in difficult times, he had had to sell a third of the farm off and, as he had seen so often in life with the decisions he had made, hindsight reviewed them poorly! His land then quickly decided to quadruple in value! This had been the man who had seen the cross and listened to Alan in Bunclody the previous day. He had reflected on some of the questions and the answers given. He needed more answers and came seeking help.

We talked through the specific dilemmas in his life and the business pressures he had faced for years and his deep-seated belief that his land was cursed. He wondered if we could pray for this farm.

We talked of many things in the farming world but God lays firm foundations. My favourite verse in the whole of God's Word is found in 3 John 2 which says, "Beloved, I pray that you may prosper in all things and be in health, just as your soul prospers" (NKJV). Often in life we can have our priorities upside down. In my experience as a pastor, many

times I have found people praying for their business and finances or their health, and yet totally neglecting their spiritual wellbeing, but that is the wrong way round, as was to be seen with this farmer. God wanted to fix a man before He would fix his land! He did. This farmer committed his life to Christ. I explained how that very day was the beginning of a whole new life for him. That day, God had made him the head not the tail. That day, God had given him a new authority over his land. With the Holy Spirit at work in his life and residing within his heart he might not even need anyone to break any curses that may or may not have rested upon his life or his land. In the short period I had to spend with him afterwards, it was evident his very language together with his demeanour had noticeably changed. **He needed answers and he got Jesus!**

Whether we like it or not, the fact is that often we, as followers of Jesus, are being observed - something that is very often unknown and unappreciated by us. How we react, what we say, how we conduct ourselves in those moments can attract seekers to God or drive them away in their hour of need. Alan passed his riot test and revival in a heart resulted.

In many cases, as the old sage once said, "We are the first Bible that many read, sometimes the only one!" Our walk is all-important.

The previous evening, we had driven up to hear the musical artist Roy Fields singing in Dublin. Roy had been involved in leading

the praise in sizeable venues in the United States of America and had indicated, in correspondence with people who knew him from Ireland, that he felt it was important to visit Ireland, particularly at this time. He believes God is doing something in our nation and it was interesting to hear an outsider's perspective on what he felt God is doing in Ireland. He intimated to the meeting that night that he felt he would be back again within the year.

We left Dublin late at night and drove through atrocious conditions. We were almost back to the caravan when we were stopped by the local Guards. The northern registration plate had attracted attention, as had my driving skills (or lack of them). Despite the driving rain, a zealous young officer enquired as to what we were up to. When he heard we were doing a cross walk and I was a pastor he said "Well, Let me preach to you!" He informed me that we were three men in a two man pick up and clearly with only two safety belts. I offered to ride the rest of the journey in the back of the pickup; he offered a seat in the police station instead! However with the persistence of the driving rain and a heart that was being melted, mercy prevailed and he allowed us to finish last few miles of a journey in the comfort of the cab. We were all very glad, especially me!

As we arrived into Baltinglass, a camera-man called Billy, who I think someone told me used to be involved with some of the television channels in his earlier career, made a video clippit of an interview with me and posted it on YouTube within the hour. I love

103

the real-time capability of modern media. Properly used it can be such a blessing.

As I walked further into town, I passed the local Garda station and saw several officers were congregated outside. I asked which one had shown mercy the previous evening to the three hoodlums from the North! A young officer indicated that he was the one that had got the prize soaking from the previous evening. We had the opportunity to chat with him and his colleagues and we parted the best of friends with forgiveness sought and kindly granted.

We had just left the town and were looking forward to a tea stop when a phone call came that was about to change my world. My mum was being recalled to the local health clinic for a 6pm meeting with a locum who was standing in for our regular doctor. My mum was taken to the clinic by my wife Denise and they would ring me back at 6.30pm. It was a long half hour.

They received the findings of the tests that had been conducted earlier in the week. Our worst fears were realised with the news that pancreatic cancer had been confirmed. This was devastating. My mum's dad, Granda Kingston, had died a very painful death with the same ailment and it had been for ever etched in my mother's memory. Against that background, my mum had been crying in the middle of the day, fearing the same.

The meeting with the locum was probably very similar to many such encounters up and down the land to-day, with the ever present threat of cancer in our midst. Every day homes receive devastating news. I hated being this far south and purposed immediately in my heart to drive north when I got the boys settled for the night. The meal was rushed and Alan, the chef that evening, was not feeling much like eating. None of us were.

The update phone call from Denise said that, whilst the start of the encounter was typical of what must happen up and down the land, the finish certainly was not. The locum, Dr Stewart, had indicated some of the treatments that would be investigated, recommended some things to do and, when the list was finally ended, Denise added the words "and pray!" Dr Stewart asked if my mum and Denise were Christians and, hearing they were, offered to pray with them in the situation. Denise said that when she had finished, mum had such a peace that everything was in God's hands and His care. Denise said it was one of the most uplifting medical interventions she had ever been privileged to be a part of. My mum never lost that peace.

We scouted out for a place to park the van up for the night to allow the boys to walk on to where we had it deposited. They would finish the last hour together as I headed north. An ideal place was very difficult to find in an area that felt strangely unwelcoming. After driving down one rather long lane with no room to turn we were forced into a reversing manoeuvre that ended up in the back of the caravan being damaged. It was a sickening thud and unusual in the fact that I had just driven forward to prevent exactly

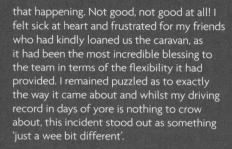

that happening. Not good, not good at all! I felt sick at heart and frustrated for my friends who had kindly loaned us the caravan, as it had been the most incredible blessing to the team in terms of the flexibility it had provided. I remained puzzled as to exactly the way it came about and whilst my driving record in days of yore is nothing to crow about, this incident stood out as something 'just a wee bit different'.

We eventually found another spot and disconnected the caravan for the night. Leaving Alan with the van, I went to locate Chris and met him coming down the road towards me. As we placed the cross in the back of the jeep, he described to me just how incredibly difficult the final stage of his walk had been. About to leave, we were approached by three men at a point called White's Cross.

The leader of the threesome had an unusual and disconcerting look about him and said he had started off life as an altar boy in Ringsend. I picked up he had lived in France for some 16 years. He walked with a swagger and it was clear amongst other things he had alcohol taken. His two scurrying henchmen, both wearing hoodies, never said a word but stood somewhat unnervingly directly behind me regardless of my attempts to counter that. Eventually they left without ever saying hello or goodbye.

As they were leaving, Chris stretched out his right hand to the man and, as their hands clasped, Chris simply said "God bless". This was met was an instant hiss sound and Chris,

despite rapidly retracting the proffered hand, said he immediately felt something like an electric shock penetrate his hand. I ushered him into the jeep and returned to where the caravan was parked. As he nursed his hand Chris said "Why did I shake his hand? I knew I shouldn't, I just knew I shouldn't!"

By the time we were all reunited I knew we had significant problems. I had two men both now being violently sick and Chris showing me his hand and saying, "I have never been bitten by a snake before but I would imagine it would feel exactly like that." Clearly visible were what, you would have to admit, looked remarkably like two fang insertion points, now very red and swollen. I have never seen a snake bite wound - all I knew was the Wicklow mountain area was presenting us with the most difficult night of the entire crosswalk to date.

Fear was very real in that place. Chris wanted, then and there, immediately to leave the Across Ireland Cross Walk team. It was almost as if fear had been injected into his bloodstream and now it had gripped his heart. I encircled them both with prayer and anointed them with oil. When we got the situation settled a fraction, we moved further north where we camped for the night. Given everything that happened, it was impossible to leave the team unsupported and without a vehicle.

I got Alan eventually to lie down in the caravan after he had been so sick literally he could be sick no more and I then spent an hour praying with Chris in the jeep. We talked

105

about the incidents of the evening, with his hand still swollen but now under the word of God - literally. After that hour of concerted prayer and focusing on key scriptures from God's word, the sense of conflict subsided. When I got everyone settled down for the night, I had an opportunity to call mum back and pray with her. It was good to hear her voice and know she was in strong spirits despite what her day had dealt her.

I went to bed exhausted thinking about the Amalekites, an enemy tribe of Israel, who Moses records in Exodus 17:8 "came and attacked the Israelites at Rephidim". This they did, without any apparent provocation during the Exodus journey from Egypt. Deuteronomy 25:17-18 sheds a little more light on the nature of the attack they unleashed: "When you were weary and worn out, they met you on your journey and attacked all who were lagging behind; they had no fear of God" (NIV). It felt that right at the end of the day, we too, thousands of years later, had been subjected to just such an Amalekite attack, only this time, the Wicklow mountains not

the wilderness was the backdrop.

We sensed a great darkness over the area. It has since come to my attention that a witch's coven holds an annual outdoor ritual in the Wicklow Mountains. That coven goes by name the 'Serpent Coven'. This was printed in several popular mainstream newspapers a couple of years later!

One might imagine that, had you known this piece of information before you walked the ground, you might have thought that your mind was playing tricks on you in our situation with an attack from the occult. But we didn't know. It wasn't until a couple of years later that the coven's existence and its name were revealed in the press! This underscores that God knows all, sees all and at times reveals things for us to pray into and take authority over.

In the middle of that night, I woke from my sleep with a single clear instruction – three words – "Write a book!"

FRIDAY 12TH AUGUST

We woke early in the morning with Alan still not feeling good, having had a very restless night. He was running a temperature and not strong enough to carry the cross. Alan described his pain on the night before as truly oppressive and unlike anything he had ever experienced. We left him feeling a little

stronger, sufficient enough to tidy the van, as we had several visitors coming down to encourage us again from the North.

Chris and I revisited the spot where the previous evening we had encountered our very unwelcome visitors. We started with communion before setting off. Chris' hand still clearly showed the marks of the previous evening's encounter but, unlike last night, today there was an assurance in his heart that through all this he was learning to overcome.

We had previously read 1 John 2:13 and 14, "I am writing to you, young men, because you have overcome the evil one...I write to you, young men, because you are strong and the word of God lives in you and you have overcome the evil one" (NIV).

The next morning the lads were talking about the fact that this has all been a bit of an adventure, with so many stories that we should write a book. They were of course joking but I was struck by this and the clear thought from the night before. I told them to just hold that thought!

The long miles continued with tired feet and a tired mind. A lady pulled up beside me and asked an odd question. There was no "hello", no "How are you doing?, no "What are you doing?" but simply the question, "Are you the same man who had stayed at my parents' house in the mid-80s?"

Well, that woke me up! Slightly puzzled, I asked her, "Why would you think that? "Well, he had a cross - oh, and long hair!" Well I suppose on one account there was a similarity - oh to have hair, let alone long hair!

She went on to tell me that in 1986 when she was a little girl, a man carrying a cross had visited her parents' house. They gave him a meal and a bed for the night and he gave

her a 50 pence piece, a grand sum of money in those days!

Two days earlier, on the Wednesday, she had talked about that 80's caller with some family friends and reminisced at length about the fact the man had given her the money. Then one of them came dashing into her house the very next day saying, "You're not going to believe what I have just seen, but there is a guy on the road WITH A CROSS!" Whilst at first she thought he was only winding her up, other neighbours confirmed that there was indeed "an eejit on the road with a cross!" And so, after a couple of decades and a couple of days she came looking.

When I told her that I had never done anything of this nature before she was intrigued. She knew there was no way I could have engineered that conversation in her home that Wednesday evening. Given that I was not someone who travelled everywhere lugging a cross behind, the fact that I should be on her very road this very week was hard for her to fathom. She said she had only ever been to one Christian meeting before and had wanted to leave early because it was 'so different'.

We talked for almost three quarters of an hour and I do remember simply saying to her that when God comes calling your way, twice, it may be prudent to consider and ask a different question "Why?" She asked herself that; she asked me that and many, many more questions.

American Physicist Isidor Isaac Rabi, who won a Nobel Prize in Physics in 1944 for his discovery of nuclear magnetic resonance used in MRI scans, attributed his success to the way his mother used to greet him when he came home from school each day - "Did you ask a good question today, Issac?" his mother would say.

This lady asked good questions, searching questions; however I was intrigued not so much by the barrage of questions but with what else I was observing as I talked with her. She had in the car with her, three little red headed children. I guessed that they were all probably less than six years of age. Have you ever known any child to sit still and be quiet for more than four minutes let alone over 40? Well, during the whole time when the lady asked and I answered, not once did the children interrupt. There was no, "Mummy, are we nearly there yet?" no, "Mummy, can I go to the toilet?" no, "Mummy, can I have some sweets please?" - all obvious, even essential, questions for children in the time I talked with their mum.

You have heard of cherubs? It was as if the Holy Spirit had just applied divine duct tape! In the quietness which was wholly unique, a young mother had a chance to think clearly of the events in her life, the call of the cross and the cost of commitment to Christ. She knew it was only God that could have orchestrated the events the way that He had.

She asked the Lord into her life and, before she left, I addressed the children and told them that that was possibly one of the most important days in their mummy's life and I thanked them for their perfect behaviour! It was an 11 out of 10 performance, assisting one of the most miraculous moments in any human being's life - the point when God comes to dwell in their heart. It only happens once - It only needs to. **As she drove off, she left me marvelling at a God who does detail like no other, detail that we so often fail to appreciate or are unable to see with the human eye.**

We stopped near the Golden Falls hydroelectric dam located on the River Liffey. We got speaking with a man who had recently been promoted to study in Rome. Father Chris was an accomplished linguist. We talked to him about his life in Rome and my 25th wedding anniversary, when Denise and I found ourselves in Rome. We had been granted permission to visit the Scavi excavation work that is going on underneath St Peter's Basilica. Whilst appreciating some of the historic claims and artefacts of the tour, including early believers' tombs and their inscriptions, I was left behind the tour group, after I got locked behind the sealing doors that preserve the site at the optimal humidity level, and found myself caught in a very unusual moment when a very powerful prayer welled up in my heart for Pope Benedict whilst directly beneath his Papal Altar. I prayed.

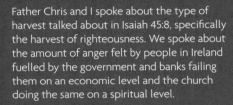

Father Chris and I spoke about the type of harvest talked about in Isaiah 45:8, specifically the harvest of righteousness. We spoke about the amount of anger felt by people in Ireland fuelled by the government and banks failing them on an economic level and the church doing the same on a spiritual level.

In the latter case, what the people we met on our travels most resented was not so much what had been allowed to happen, in what should have been safe settings for anyone, not least the most vulnerable, but the outrageous fact that the problem was covered up for so long.

Despite the pain I saw on my journey, there is still a belief in God and openness to prayer. We prayed with Father Chris and gave him our card with the two key verses on it. The land in Vatican City is as needful of the twin harvest of salvation and righteousness as any other land on this planet. David stated in Psalm 24:1 that "The Earth is the Lord's", I pray that Ireland too will be reclaimed.

The 'girl power' team from the North, consisting of Gillian, Claire and Lynne (and later Lynne's husband Johnny) again arrived to encourage. Again, almost exactly as when the girls had arrived in Sligo on Midsummer's day, their arrival was timely in terms of encouragement. They also brought down a new light cover to replace the one on the back to the caravan that we had modified the previous evening!

A lunch alongside one of the reservoirs that fed Dublin city with water and the backdrop of the mountains all made for a pleasant break.

Songs of praise from the fresh-footed high-spirited recruits as we arrived in Blessington and our second very loud blowout on the cross wheel, we took to be entirely coincidental!

It was good to have their company and their help to carry the cross. At one point, not long after the team had arrived that day, I was walking a section with Lynne when she suggested "You should write a book!" Easy for her to say! The point nonetheless was made and the point again noted, for the third time in 24hours.

It was fully teatime until Alan was feeling well enough to do his first lift of the day. We were all glad to see him back up and running again. This team was so lean we could not afford to be a man down! We together finished the first half of the long, long leg, just South of Dublin with the final 2 miles that night taking us into Saggart.

We packed up and headed for a caravan park near Dublin. The management were incredibly obliging with a discounted rate for the team on their site for the weekend. We camped overnight and enjoyed the luxury of warm showers, which soothed tired legs and arms. We were in bed by 10.45pm on a Friday night, unheard of for me, but I slept well despite the constant noise of N7 traffic on the move. As I nodded off to sleep, I thought of all those people on their way West and to Limerick, I thought back to some of the earlier comments at the start of this Leg and imagined great changes by God of Irish hearts and to see them pouring eastwards out of Wexford to Europe – 'peregrinatio pro Dei amore' wandering for the love of God. More and more that phrase burns within me – as I went to sleep I prayed for as many European countries as I could possibly think of.

SATURDAY 13TH AUGUST

The next morning before we broke back North so I could take the Sunday service in our church in Richhill, Alan and myself were afforded a slot on the morning programme of Spirit FM Radio, Ireland's first national Christian radio station. We received a warm welcome at their Dublin Studio and a terrific opportunity to share with their listeners the significance and power of God's word for people's lives in Ireland, right here, right now.

We found our way out of the city to the M1 and headed for home. I have never worked out why different Armagh men talk about going "up to Dublin" when it clearly is down to Dublin from Armagh, on all the maps I ever looked at! I could however accept that when you left from Kilmore Quays you indeed were going "up to Dublin". After a long week on foot it mattered little, but it seemed a pleasant thought to toy with that it was downhill all the way home!

One final push to go...

Armagh

Castleblaney

Ardee

Slane

Balbriggan

Ashbourne

Dublin City Centre

Saggart

Show me the way to go home!

CROSS WALK LEG 4
Continued

SUNDAY 14TH AUGUST

We left Richhill directly after the service on Sunday night and travelled back down to Dublin where we stayed once again at the campsite where we had parked up for the weekend. When we had arrived there on the Friday we had prayed with one of the site managers, before she finished her shift. When we asked what she wanted us to pray for, she said not to pray for the prosperity of their business but rather that they would be better people. We prayed for her and her boss that the campsite staff would pick up on the needs of people and that this place would become a haven to help and support people who came from far off fields to visit Dublin and stay with them. We left thanking the team for their hospitality.

MONDAY 15TH AUGUST

We picked up our walk where we left off in Saggart and the final leg began with the longest conversation I had with any individual on the entire five weeks of this epic journey. We spoke with a man who told us how, as a child, he had lost a hand in an accident. As he described to us the horrors of the incident we were stunned to hear him say that it wasn't the worst thing that could have happened to anyone. He told us how the pursuit of money led him to build a successful business, which he had opportunely offloaded just before the recession. He talked about how he was always looking for the next thing, always buying the latest gadget; never satisfied. He truly believed in living

for the moment, just for right now. So many people that I have seen believe the same false mantra, but unfortunately many have not been fortunate enough to have sold at the top of the market and negative equity is now not just a term but a daunting reality for many.

What do you give a man who has got everything?
The man claimed he owned half of Saggart. All I knew was that he owned a restaurant in town, but because it was a Monday it was unfortunately closed. A coffee would have been nice for a dry throat! I gave him the only thing we had of value - one of the Bibles we

had in the jeep. He had talked to me about the significance of the 'now' moment where we, as human beings, have a chance to choose and that those choices seriously impact on each individual's future. It is often said, "life is short, live for the moment!" but what about, "eternity is long, prepare for it!" I thought about his future and his eternity and prayed that he would read and connect with the truth contained within those priceless pages.

As I left the man and set off again, it took considerable time for me to catch up with the team. We were now moving towards the centre of Dublin. Alan and Chris had had several encounters on the outskirts of the city. The previous evening we had taken stock of the amount of cards we had to hand out to people who engaged with us. Given the quantity we had distributed on the previous three and a half legs, we felt we were going to find ourselves well short, bearing in mind we were about to walk into the largest city in Ireland with almost two million people living in the greater Dublin area. Sadly, our fears proved wholly unfounded. In the city whose name is derived from the Irish Dubh Linn, meaning "dark/black pool", the going was tough and encounters were sparse. Occasionally we engaged with the homeless but, by and large, the vast majority of people in this great metropolis passed by on the other side.

Not far from a public art sculpture depicting homelessness on the streets of Dublin, I sat and spoke with a group of homeless people, including James and Carol. A guy called Billy came along asking if they could read or write.

Carol admitted that she could not. Billy asked why they were out on the street, indicating that there were enough hostels for anyone suffering homelessness in the capital and there was no need for anyone to be suffering on the street.

He then asked me a very pertinent question in their hearing, "What can Jesus do for these people?" I told them I liked his tense! I said Jesus was interested in them and so we must be too. I had no money on me but if I had, I could have shared it. I said I would be expected to share my coat but they were already all wearing one and were as well attired as me, but I could pray and did. Billy gave them some Virginia tobacco and roll ups to afford them a smoke.

As I left with him and we walked together a while, we discussed practical Christianity — what Jesus would do in that setting. Whilst proffering someone a cigarette might not receive the blessing of any health department, let alone Jesus, I told him that he had shared what he had. **It was the only act of concern I saw that day in an all-too-busy city.**

As we walked, I shared with Billy something that my old Pastor, Jim, had shared with me the first night I met him. He ranked five priorities of a man as he saw it. I told Billy I always like when someone speaks simply to me. Whilst many men are at different stages of their life, the list is still pertinent and it is something I never forgot:

1. His relationship with God
2. His wife
3. His children
4. His spiritual home
5. His job

God: Pastor Jim said that the most important thing in a man's life was his personal relationship with the living God. A man needs to find out what on earth he is here for and to understand what his Designer designed him for.

Our wives: He said we have to take care of our wives, as well in private as we do in public. He used to be a policeman in Glasgow and sometimes he saw, for example, a couple with the husband's arm around his wife at 3pm as they attended a wedding reception. At 3am the following morning he was scraping the same woman off a wall as result of the husband's alcohol abuse!

Our children: If we are blessed enough to be entrusted with young lives to lead and guide and mentor, we should do it well.

Our spiritual home: We need to be there and invest time in the lives of the people we worship with.

Our work: We need to do it well.

Having established the order, Pastor Jim said that the arch enemy of our souls has always attacked and tried to reverse God's order wherever and whenever he could. When God put things the right way up the enemy tries to reverse it and turn a man's world upside down. He takes a young man and makes his career and work the be-all-and-end-all of life. He tramps over anyone and everyone to get to the top, only to find when he is at the top of the ladder, just as American businessman Dr. Stephen Covey once pointed out, that the ladder was unfortunately up against the wrong wall! Indeed, Dr Covey, in his most popular book "The 7 Habits of Highly Effective People" (1998) points out that if our ladder is not leaning against the right wall, every step we take just gets us to the wrong place faster!

If the enemy could not tie a man up with his career and money, he would have him doing charitable deeds; collecting money for Tear Fund or Trócaire, painting a chapel or church wall - it looked good on the outside but that wasn't the foremost priority.

If he could not tie a man up with his career, his charitable deeds or his church, he would try and tie him up with his family - being a great father to them.

The very last thing the enemy ever wanted to see any man getting right was the 'main thing'. Dr. Stephen Covey in many of his motivational lectures and books often asserted that in business as in life, 'the main thing is to keep the main thing, the main thing'; in this case a man's personal relationship with his Creator.

Billy and I said our goodbyes; he admitted that sadly for him it was all too late, at least at one level - he was now divorced. We parted and the push North continued.

Five Evertonians, over for a pre-season friendly, mocked the cross. Two walked in front and one jeeringly stated to his mate, "Hey! Jesus is following us!" I smiled and suggested to them "Should it not be the other way around?" I could tell from their changed and now softer demeanour, that they knew they had encountered truth. They got the point and soon we too got to The Point, in O'Connell Street, Dublin's busiest thoroughfare. We stopped to pray in the centre of the capital city of Ireland, outside the General Post Office (GPO), where Patrick Pierce made his famous speech and the assertion that the young Irish men needed to shed their blood and die, if need be, to save Ireland. Only one man ever died to save Ireland – his name is Jesus.

Praying Isaiah 45:8 on the footpath outside the GPO in O'Connell Street proved bizarrely easier said than done. The team had lost count of how many occasions in the centre of towns and villages these now ingrained Scriptures had been prayed. Nevertheless, praying that day in Dublin was difficult. I found the thoughts and the words, which normally flowed so readily, seemed hard to formulate and stuck to the roof of my mouth. It felt like a senior moment, a mental blank and as if had just been to the dentist all rolled up in one! Odd, but given the difficulty of the terrain we felt we had walked that day, hardly surprising.

As we exited the city northward, we talked of times as a team when the cross had felt unusually heavy physically and comments that had been particularly scathing. It had indeed felt a dark day, possibly the darkest of the entire walk to date. One final encounter before leaving the city environs was, however, one that I would not forget. Chris came and pulled me out of the jeep to meet a man called Michael, probably around 60 years of age, and his dog, Sam, who sat in the pannier basket on the front of his old bicycle.

I listened as he shared his heart for his people. He spoke of North and South together spiritually. He talked of the Word and the Spirit successfully combined and flowing together to create a powerful mix which spread beyond the shores. He spoke our language.

He talked of the moment when her Majesty Queen Elizabeth II had bowed her head in the Garden of Remembrance, during her recent historic visit a few months earlier in May. Michael described it as a "grace-filled moment".

The Garden of Remembrance is a large sunken garden with a water feature in the shape of the cross. The floor of the cross is lined with mosaics of shattered swords and broken shields - echoing the rituals of ancient clans who would break their weapons at the end of battle and throw them into the rivers or large bodies of water to symbolize the end of a conflict.

Michael went on to talk about the Queen's visit to Cork, an area famed for its fierce independence and yet where the sense of joy and celebration pervaded the visit in the South West - something unthinkable not so very long ago.

He talked about two groups that were right there and then in Dublin "cursing the city". This man spoke clearly, his choice of words both considered and unusually informed; he seemed to have his finger on the pulse of the city for which he was clearly concerned. I asked if he would allow us to pray with him for his city. He agreed. I took his hand and unlike in O'Connell Street, this time the prayer and the verses flowed with ease. I had just finished Isaiah 45:8 and only just embarked on the much shorter Jeremiah 22:29 verse, when the heavens opened in a phenomenal downpour. We parted from this kind old man so rapidly we hardly had time to say goodbye in order to allow both him, and us, to grab shelter. As we watched the heavens empty like never before, I felt we had met someone unique. There was something about his character, something about the prayer, something about the timing of the torrent then falling all around that left me wondering just exactly who we had been talking to.

As mentioned before, earlier in the walk we initially had seen rain as a trial, but in this case it was the total opposite as we pondered that something in the physical realm might mirror what was happening in the spiritual. One spectacularly splendid soaking saved our day!

Once again the prophecies that I initially read on the Strangford shoreline came back to me. One was a contribution from Dennis Cramer and others dated back to 1997.

Ireland and Northern Ireland: Healing, Wholeness and Happiness
In this troubled corner of the world, God will work perhaps one of His greatest miracles! The masterful, yet evil diversion of the devil that has kept this region smouldering in hatred, bitterness and resentment will finally be exposed, and mercy drops will fall. The battle for men's souls can and will be won!

Laughing together again
Like long lost brothers who have been supernaturally reunited, Ireland and Northern Ireland will laugh together again. It will not be a nervous or artificial or phoney laugh. Instead, brothers will share laughter from deep down inside. It will be laughter of release from centuries of tension and strife. Even the soil, the physical ground, will sigh with relief - such will be the deliverance of this people. The awful physical, emotional and spiritual wound will finally be healed by the supernatural hand of God. The history of tribal violence, with its lust for bloodshed and its insatiable hunger for death, will come to an end. This ancient demon will rear its ugly head no more. The Son of Righteousness will arise with healing in His wings. God will exercise His great jealousy over this region and will ransom it for the Kingdom of God. Get ready, for it will happen suddenly!

Rain for a dry people
Ireland will experience an unpredictable
chain of events - half meteorological and half supernatural - that will suddenly awaken this land. Like torrential showers, God's Spirit will rain down upon this spiritually dry people. Revival will break out in the countryside and in the cities - among the rich and the poor, with Catholics and Protestants. Churches will overflow with converts, and people will literally run to churches to experience repentance and salvation. Many ministers will be overwhelmed and will flee, hoping to escape this wonderful yet terrible revival. God will not be limited and He will shake the established religious order of this land. It will be everything the people had hoped for and everything they had feared. Names and titles, denominations and organizations will take a back seat to this wonderful, yet seemingly out-of-control, revival. Even Ireland's government officials will publicly acknowledge this incredible manifestation of the Holy Spirit. It will be undeniable. A **drastic increase in physical rainfall over this region will signify an increased outpouring of God's Spirit. This will be a healing rainfall and a cleansing downpour upon the people. God will cleanse the land both physically and spiritually as physical rains and spiritual rains fall from the heavens simultaneously.** *Streams and rivers will deepen and widen, overflowing their banks, as their waters announce this unprecedented visitation from God. God says to Ireland, "Look up, for your redemption draws nigh."*

As we left the city that day, the rain was so intense and so prolonged that we videoed, for the first time, the Cross Walk beneath the raining down Heavens

119

TUESDAY 16TH AUGUST

On Tuesday morning we continued our walk north and said goodbye to Dublin. Unlike the previous day, encounters with the general public grew in frequency and openness. I met a lady who was a bookkeeper who had a great heart for the disadvantaged, a restaurant owner called Seammie who encouraged us to call into his restaurant further on up the road for a bite to eat. Conversation after conversation flowed freely. By the time we did get to the aforementioned restaurant we were greeted by Seammie's wife who said her husband had phoned ahead and our meal was "on the house."

Three massive shepherd's pies, three Cokes and some good old fashioned Irish hospitality was very welcome, especially as Chris had said earlier that for some reason he was "starving". Their shepherd's pie hit the spot perfectly! We talked over lunch about each of our experiences on the road – how significantly different the engagements with people now were. I asked if we had recently crossed any specific rivers or boundaries; Alan said he thought we had – "a wee one called the Ward River". Whatever the cause, the spiritual atmosphere felt very different from Dublin and much more refreshing. As we parted with the restaurant owners we thanked them and prayed for them and their business.

Further north, in Ashbourne we met a retired quantity surveyor, formerly a Limavady man, who had moved there some 40-odd years ago. He had a great interest in the spiritual history of Ireland; in particular he had organised visits and trips covering the sites

of significance to St. Canice, who followed a couple of hundred years after St. Patrick. We related some of our experiences over the previous couple of days and in conversation I asked about the Ward River. He informed us that that was the boundary between Co. Dublin and Co. Meath.

We made good progress that day and it was that time of the evening where the logistics manager was attempting to locate a place to set up camp for the night. Just then a gentleman stopped me and informed me he was a born again Christian and asked if I needed anything. A place to park please!

It was certainly no accident that we met this man! We were welcomed by him to his bungalow nearby and, after we parked up, the boys relaxed in the caravan as I listened to something of our host's story. He shared how he had cried out to God one night when he was in absolute desperation and despair and contemplating ending his life. It is an extraordinary miracle when God takes the old and makes all things new. God's salvation of a human soul was so real – here was a man was sitting on exactly the same settee, in the same home, in the same county and country but the whole world had changed! Indeed more than that, because he described the sense of peace that he had begun to experience as literally "out of this world." He was now studying at Bible College, having resigned his role as a marketing director with one of the leading drug companies in Ireland.

In the midst of him sharing something of the pain and joy that was his life, we heard much merriment outside in the garden. A short time later the boys entered the house with tears in their eyes saying, "Pastor we did all we could!" We had no idea what had been going on until Alan furnished us the pictorial evidence that would explain everything. Apparently, or so their story went, a stray dog had arrived in the garden, let itself into the caravan, climbed six feet, opened a cupboard, stole a cellophane inner liner of Jaffa Cakes from MY stash and made off down the garden path before either of them could apprehend the scoundrel!

A likely tale my host thought. Me? I knew there was much more to it! There was clearly enticement, jealousy, collusion, aiding and abetting, temptation and causing a weaker one to sin to name but a few and all that set against a background of slothful stewardship not to mention betrayal!

The Worried Watchmen!

The thief comes to steal...

and escape...

121

It was a crime of the highest order and made participation in the group Bible Study in Balbriggan difficult to concentrate upon until supper arrived with the consolation of freshly made Rice Krispie buns!

Meeting with that small group of believers from Balbriggan was very special. The leader of the group shared how, since he had taken over the oversight of the church, domestic pressure and the spiritual onslaught against his family had increased significantly. As a team we spent the night talking and praying together with them and for what God was doing in their midst.

WEDNESDAY 17TH AUGUST

In the morning, I awoke early to spend time with our host. Since we had met him, I sensed something in my heart saying that this man has significance in the kingdom of heaven as a man of influence and leadership.

That contrasted sharply against a domestic setting where the dogs seemed to exert their will upon their master rather than the other way around. In order to return his kindness for the use of his home the previous evening, Alan spent some time talking to him about dog training and as a group we weeded the drive in front of his house - I wanted to help bring about some small physical change to the land we been had invited onto and prayed over the evening before.

Why Would Anyone...
We packed up and were soon back on the road once again. As I walked, a lady called Geraldine pulled up beside me. She stopped to say that she had seen me on the way to the airport a couple of hours earlier and I had "bugged" her all morning. Somewhat surprised I enquired, "Bugged you? In what way?" She explained that when had been

He could understand on a hot day such as the one we were currently walking in, that someone buy me water for refreshment and a Mars bar for energy but who in their right mind brings you a single inner cellophane liner from a packet of Jaffa Cakes?

Some random options for the situation: Someone that collects limited edition Jaffa Cake outers?
Unlikely!

Someone who is ecologically friendly and wants to win a prize for County Cardboard Recycling Champion?
Again unlikely!

Someone that does not want to see unnecessary litter dropped in the local countryside?
Possibly!

Just another one of those inexplicable coincidences?
Too many on this trip!

Someone who, unknown to them, was being used to replace exactly what had been stolen the night before – an inner cellophane liner of Jaffa Cakes?
Hmmm!

leaving her daughter to catch a flight and saw me on the road she wondered if this strange man had had anything at all to eat or drink, especially given it was such a warm day. She drove all the way to Dublin airport, deposited her daughter and drove back up the road. In the interim she had stopped off somewhere and had bought me a bottle of water, a Mars bar and yes you guessed it... a packet of Jaffa Cakes! However, this time there was an intriguing difference with the Jaffa Cakes. She presented me with an inner cellophane liner of Jaffa Cakes – no cardboard box outer, just the inner sleeve!

I thanked Geraldine profusely and set out grinning like a Cheshire cat that had the cream. When I caught up with Chris he looked with bemusement at the three gifts. **Many centuries ago, an on-time delivery of gold, frankincense and myrrh by the three wise men carried significance, this delivery by just one wise woman from Ireland left Chris more than a little mystified!**

Chris knew not, but what he did know was that again and again, so very many times on this trip he had watched extraordinary provision at significant times.

Less than two hours later, for example, we happened upon some members of a Camera

123

Club for people with Down's Syndrome who were on a day's outing to Slane to practice their photography skills. I felt prompted to buy them an ice cream, so we gave their leader €20 to do just that. Within 10 minutes of that encounter, Peter Aiken our church secretary in Richhill had travelled down to see how we were getting along and encourage us on our way. He arrived with €20 "for an ice cream" - one of those little inexplicable coincidences? Chris was beginning to see on this Cross Walk an irrefutable mountain of evidence stacking against that as a credible option! I leave it to you the reader to fill in the blank. All I know is I enjoyed the Jaffa Cakes a lot! Thank you Geraldine!

We continued on our way to the next objective, the Hill of Slane. As I neared town, I met Patrick Heron, an author with whom I had a very enjoyable discussion that centred primarily on his current areas of interest in the Bible. We discussed, in the first book of Genesis, the appearance of the Nephilim and also one of Patrick's books "Return of the Antichrist". It was interesting to put the face behind the pen. The cross crossed the Boyne and made the long climb up to the top of hill

of Slane. That mile I managed to miss carrying the cross! Thank you Patrick...a lot!

It was here at the Hill of Slane that, many centuries earlier, Patrick allegedly lit a fire that proved to be very significant.

Long established tradition tells that St. Patrick lit the Easter Fire on this Hill of Slane in 433. In doing so, he unwittingly disobeyed King Laoghaire at nearby Tara.

The inevitable confrontation had a happy outcome: Laoghaire's druid, Erk, became a Christian (later, first Bishop of Slane) and the King was pacified.

The Easter Fire is still lighted, each year, on the Hill of Slane.

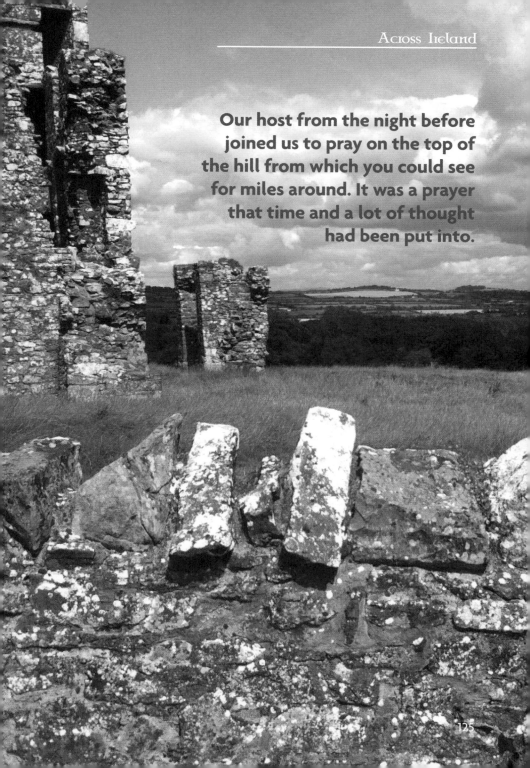

Our host from the night before joined us to pray on the top of the hill from which you could see for miles around. It was a prayer that time and a lot of thought had been put into.

Before we parted, he did one final job for me...

At an earlier point, when we were still south of Dublin I asked the team "What is THE river in Ireland?" Chris suggested it was the River Bann (probably given the fact that he lived beside it and had just recently lost a dear friend to suicide in it). Alan said, "The Shannon – it's the longest!" As for me, I was actually thinking of the River Boyne – so much for team unity! Alan asked why I was asking the question.

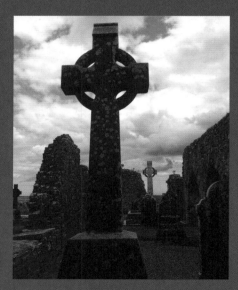

During this last leg of the Cross Walk, my daily readings from the Bible were centred in the book of Exodus, the story of Moses leading God's people Israel out of bondage in Egypt. As God unveiled his plan and

assurances to Moses right at the outset, God instructed Him, amongst other things, to "take water from the river and pour it on the dry land. The water which you take from the river will become blood on the dry land" (Exodus 4:9b, NKJV).

The significance and the all-encompassing spread of God's power was evidenced when Aaron was told ... "stretch out your hand over the waters of Egypt, over their streams, over their rivers, over their ponds, and over all their pools of water, that they may become blood. And there shall be blood throughout all the land of Egypt, both in buckets of wood and pitchers of stone" (Exodus 7:19, NKJV).

It wasn't just Pharaoh who saw the impact of that instruction being carried out in obedience; every single home that day felt the impact; every single home saw stored water reserves appear as blood in their house; every single home. Since reading the story, the all-encompassing effect of every home being impacted struck me and stayed with me.

Rivers had grown in their significance for us on our journey and so, with the simple thought that we might, in some way, reflect our desire for every home in the entire nation of Ireland to be impacted positively with the message of God's love and power, our host collected a five gallon drum of the Boyne River's famous flow and gave it to us as we said goodbye so that we could pour it on the land at Navan Fort when we arrived at our final destination, symbolising the blessing that we wanted to rain out on the land, impacting upon every home.

126

SUPPORTERS SUPPORTING

Alan came across two young people in their late teens on the other side of the road as he walked. They crossed over to talk to him. Kevin carried the cross enthusiastically with Alan after being offered the opportunity to do so. Together they talked as they walked - their understanding of all things faith; sin and salvation, life and death, Heaven and Hell. The young man said he had no concerns about going to Hell. When Alan asked if God would let him into Heaven he responded quite easily in the affirmative. As Alan shared, Kevin started to realise that his god might let him automatically into heaven but that was not the God of the Bible. When he started to learn of the value of a human soul, the enormous price that had to be paid to counter his sin, what Jesus had gone through for him on the cross, he all of a sudden and quite unexpectedly for him, was faced with

a choice. His god and the God of the Bible seemed poles apart in terms of what they expected and what they both gave as a result.

Alan was just about to leave when Kevin said, "I want to do it!" and that day he surrendered his life to the one and only true and living God adding, "I want to be a better man."

Another moment. Another miracle. **Another Man United Supporter!**

Many of the folks along this long journey we may well not have the opportunity to meet again but, as God answers Kevin's prayer to "make him a better man," I trust one of the first things to be positively impacted is his dress sense – ditch the football shirt! It would appear God is still a God of grace!

THURSDAY 18TH AUGUST

Early that morning as I arrived in Ardee, a tidy town, my first conversation was with a tyre changer who was getting set up for his day changing tyres and fixing punctures. After he heard something of our Across Walk journey, conversation naturally gravitated round to something that he knew more about than I did. People like that for me are very easy to find! In life it is good to listen and learn from other people's stories. His area of expertise? Tyres naturally. He certainly didn't believe me when I said that we had two blowouts on our single wheeled cross! He said quite categorically, "That's impossible!" Well, if

nothing else, he too learned something new that morning.

Maybe they just sell better tyres in Ardee than Armagh!

That day saw a visit from the Rev Ian Cruickshank, from Kilkenny - an old friend of Alan's who came for most of the day. We were also graced with members of Richhill Elim Church to join the team, share the load and support us along the way!

We had Paul Thompson, Dougie Treverton and his big son Josh (the best dressed man on the day by a mile) to help us out. Eddie and Doris also arrived to help, with a pot of stew and an apple tart and, to top it all off, lashings of ice cream and jelly to enjoy that afternoon.

It was good to have all the gang for the day! We made rapid progress, given all the fresh legs and boundless enthusiasm, and the fellowship was wonderful. When eventually we settled down to have a take-away in the caravan, everyone indicated they had thoroughly enjoyed the day and not least the wonderful provisions which Doris and Eddie furnished us with. Thank you all!

Around teatime, a white van pulled up and the driver wanted to talk with me. He introduced himself as Paul and I recognised him from Leg 1 of our journey and the town of Monaghan. Paul had been involved in weekend street outreach for quite a few years in Monaghan and he wanted to share his experiences since we last met and together prayed Isaiah 45:8 in his town, at the spot where George Jeffreys preached all those years ago. Since that day, his street work changed. Late into the night, where revellers

previously had no time for the gospel, the past six weeks had seen a softening in hearts and a marked openness to prayer that he had never witnessed before.

He was the only one we spoke to on the cross walk who had the advantage of a clear 'before and after' Isaiah 45:8 perspective that gave him a degree of objectivity. He was thankful to be there that day and genuinely excited at what future was beginning to look like. All I can say is that we are not called to be successful but to be faithful. All I know is that I saw a genuine guy, with a heart after God and for the lost, seriously encouraged and motivated in his faith. Praise the Lord. The power of the cross!

On our travels across Ireland we stayed in many varying locations but tonight, our final night on the road, the logistics manager excelled himself and, a bit like the wedding in Cana, the best was kept until last. Alan dropped us into the most beautiful lakeside setting you could imagine in Castleblaney. It was wonderful.

THE LAST DAY – FRIDAY 19TH AUGUST

For the duration of the time on the road I was consigned to the far end of the caravan and every morning the first thing I awoke to see was the caravan door... but not on that last Friday morning.

I awoke just before dawn and sat studying with the top half of the stable-style door open.

We were in the grounds of 'Hope Castle', as it was called, though even in its heyday it was probably more a mansion or manor house.

The Hope family's ownership of the estate gave not only our camping spot its name but also their world renowned family heirloom, the 'Hope Diamond', the largest of its kind in the world and said to be the second most-visited artwork in the world, after the Mona Lisa.

Such a setting was ideal when I was mulling through what we had hoped to achieve over that summer — initially a walk of some 430 miles seemed improbable but now here we were, by the grace of God, on the final day.

I thought of others who had seen through far more weightier projects than Across Ireland had done, Old Testament leaders who were involved in projects that lasted some time, like Moses. Whilst the Bible doesn't say precisely, some commentators think it may have taken as much as a year from the first plague began until the final release of the children of Israel from their bondage. Eventually the final night and the final plague came and the Passover was observed before the slaves were set free. Exodus records some things God said just prior to it: "I will execute judgment against all the gods of Egypt, for I am the Lord!" and "This is a day to remember" (Exodus 12:12 and 14, NLT)

His successor Joshua followed the divine battle strategy that led to the capture of Jericho. This was significantly shorter. In the final build-up before Jericho was taken, Joshua chapter six records that after all the preparations and walking around the city of Jericho was completed, it then to came to the culmination of what they were working toward. It says, "On the 7th day the Israelites got up at dawn and marched around the town as they had done before" (Joshua 6:15, NLT).

Whilst technically I didn't get up, I sat in the sleeping bag and watched dawn develop. It was stunning and from time to time I tried to capture the early light on that final day.

This, the last day of our walk, was certainly a day to remember and this seemed to be echoed in the sunrise on that final morning.

A LOST SHEEP

We set off on our final march north. A lorry driver stopped with me. His name was Dave and he was from North Wales, a place I knew well after studying at University College of North Wales (UCNW). Again, as happened so many times on this journey, I find myself faced with a person who is more than a little puzzled at their own behaviour. Dave queried me, but much more he addressed this question to himself - "I drive thousands of miles every week and I never stop on the side of the road like this! What am I doing?"

Whilst apparently unhelpful, I excused myself for 7-8 minutes to speak to a family who interrupted asking about what we were doing, but this afforded Dave an opportunity to attempt to answer his own rhetorical question. Despite the delay, Dave remained where he was and the question remained unanswered. When I got back to him the rain had started to fall more heavily and I suggested we step under a tree as we continued our conversation. As we stepped under its welcome cover, I simply had the impression I should tell him the story of Zacchaeus who climbed a tree to find Jesus – the very fact that Zacchaeus was so keen to meet the son of God he climbed up a tree, had me wondering if it was anything like the size of this one. Was this also a demonstration of the similarity of God's drawing power this time with Dave?

I had no sooner started speaking, when Dave had his hands up to his ears shouting at me to stop! I asked what was going on with him and he said he couldn't work out what was

happening! "Why on earth are you talking about Zacchaeus?" he asked. Whilst his Grandfather's name was Zachariah, for reasons he had never fully understood, his family and friends always referred to him as Zacchaeus! He said he was tingling from head to toe! God simply used ONE name to open up his heart to the good news about Jesus's death for Dave.

It was clear God was at work. I asked Dave a simple question, "What if a red van came round that corner and hit us and we both arrived in eternity and God asked the question, "Dave why should I let you into my Heaven?" (Several times I had listened to R.T. Kendal in the Waterfront and at Hillsborough Bible Week pose that very question).

Dave's response? - "Cause I was standing talking to a holy man of God!" His answer hung hopefully in the air awaiting a response. Nice try but I guess it showed how little he knew we all need a Saviour, not least me and no doubt, when he had some more time to reflect on it, he would see what an incredibly weak line of argument that might be to hang your whole eternity upon.

A few minutes later, he actually startled me by shouting "There's the red van!" He wasn't joking either, but thankfully it left us where we were, with still just a little more time to consider the importance of what we had both been discussing together. It was a sobering, thought-provoking moment for two men at the side of a road that day in Ireland.

After we had spoken for a long time and I had fielded more of his questions, he was ready and wanted to make his peace with God but he wanted to pray in his own words in his own way. I was not sure if it was shyness or not but he climbed back into his driver's seat. As he left, again he said, "Normally I would never, ever have stopped to ask a random stranger on the side of the road all these questions. I am just a "lost sheep" driving around the road network of Europe."

I have no idea how many miles of road network do actually exist in Europe, probably an extraordinary statistic; but that day, on that ordinary road in Ireland, one lone lorry driver did something he never did; stopped and questioned where he was headed on the road of his life. No matter the twists and turns in that road, no matter how long the road runs, it would one day come to the inevitable T-Junction. Would he turn right and be put

amongst the sheep on the right or would he turn to the left and end up with the goats there?

That choice, as with us all, was his alone. Probably the most precious gift God has entrusted to lorry drivers and farmers and housewives and teachers and scientists and politicians and men and women and children is the freedom to choose what you will do with the gift of salvation that God is offering.

I gave him a Bible and prayed that Jesus would complete the work that only He can; as the Good Shepherd rescuing one lost sheep who had strayed a long, long way from his home near the Snowdonian mountains. Dave left with his new bible and a new understanding in his heart of a God who had always loved him. He received real road-side assistance to help in his journey through life! It was an extraordinary day.

AT LONG LAST

We eventually made it for the fourth and final time to Navan Fort where we met Andy with guitar and Gordon with shofar, a centuries old musical instrument made from a ram's horn. On previous occasions we simply ascended the mound from the direction we had walked from, first West, next North, next East and now finally from the South. However this time before we did, we rounded the mound six times, just as Joshua had, and on the seventh, with the shofar blowing as in times

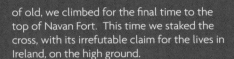

of old, we climbed for the final time to the top of Navan Fort. This time we staked the cross, with its irrefutable claim for the lives in Ireland, on the high ground.

The cross had done every single mile - the full length and breadth of our entire land sea to sea, through wind and rain.

We released the water from "the river" around the foot of the cross that did all that work. We read, amongst other things, a verse from Jeremiah 49:2 "Therefore, behold, the days are coming, declares the LORD, when I will cause the battle cry to be heard... it shall become a desolate mound, ...then Israel shall dispossess those who dispossessed him, says the LORD" (ESV).

For the fourth and final time we prayed Isaiah 45:8 Jeremiah 22:29 on that mound.

We simply want to see our enemy dispossessed. The thief comes to steal our land, our hearts our minds and rob God of the glory He rightfully deserves from worshipping hearts in Ireland.

Andy had put those now familiar words of what we had prayed so often, in every town and village we walked through in Ireland, to music and there we had a time of praise and of celebration for what God has done.

The long walk was over... finally.

CROSS WALK LEG 4:
Kilmore Quays, Wexford to Navan Fort | 195 miles

Reflections

Having completed our journey, the sentiment of an elderly, unnamed Grandmother (as recorded in Martin Luther King's autobiography by Clayborne Carson) struck a chord with me: "...So profoundly had the spirit of protest become a part of people's lives, sometimes they even preferred to walk even when a ride was available. The act of walking, for many, had become of symbolic importance. Once a pool driver stopped beside an elderly woman who trudging along with obvious difficulty. "Jump in, Grandmother," he said. "You don't need to walk." She waved him on. "I'm not walking for myself," she explained, "I am walking for my children and my grandchildren," and she continued toward home.

Although we can understand little of the burdens that had faced this community for generations, through our journey we too were allowed a small glimpse into the significant act of simply walking. We want our land and our world to be blessed for all who walk with us and behind us.

At the end of a journey such as this, one could pontificate at length about lessons learned, make great pronouncements about what comes next. I have none of those.

For me, this one picture says it all.

It was taken at Navan Fort at the end of the Across Ireland Cross Walk journey. The thing that most appealed to me was the fact that the cross stands high, the cross stands tall, the cross stands alone. **This walk was never about an individual, never about a dream team, never ever about a denomination. It was always and only about one power; the power of God, the only power that can rescue a life, redeem a soul and bring restoration to a nation.**

Where was His power and His love displayed? On a cross, some 2000 years ago, when a man came to die. The Roman Empire, at the height of its power, crucified thousands of men, all today nameless, save one – Jesus of Nazareth.

Why is his name recalled whilst so many others are forgotten? What is the significance of the Name that is above every name?

Matthew 1:21 states "...you shall call his name Jesus, for he will save his people from their sins" (ESV)

His birth, His life, His death, His resurrection, even His name all bear testimony that this was no ordinary man.

There only ever was and is and ever will be one Jesus Christ.

There is only one cross - His

There is only one church in Ireland – His

There is only one name given under Heaven whereby we must be saved – His
How should we respond?

Only in the bottom left corner of the photograph can be seen a single hand, of someone nameless, raised in praise to God for what He has achieved on the cross for me, for the team, for the people of Ireland, North South East and West.

Final Thought

As I finished writing this book at midnight on the 23rd of April,
I pondered once again on the significance of the very tight
completion date.

Perhaps, it was the fact that it was St George's Day and his famous
emblem was the cross. Perhaps, it was because that date also marked
the original date of World Book & Copyright Day but I very much
doubted that the international reading world had arranged their
annual calendar to receive my token attempt at a tale!

Perhaps it was to capture memories, whilst still very fresh in my
mind?
Perhaps, the answer lay closer to home...
That very evening I had gone to visit my Dad, who informed me that
the swallows had just arrived that day - the 23rd. He said "They came
last year on the 24th, but this year, they were a day early". I asked
how on earth he remembered such precise calendar detail and he
responded, "Your Mum used to journal their arrival every single year".
He added the observation that, within 30 minutes of their arrival,
they began to busy themselves building nests to raise their young
and to nurture and prepare them for the long return trip.

As I left, on the drive back home, I mused on our conversation; might
it one day be that international travellers, like our swallows, would
come to these shores and find a land, busy and thriving, as it again
nurtures its visitors with spiritual encouragement and sustenance
whilst here and with something significant to share with them bless
their home nations upon their return.